L
SPEAK AND WRITE
HINDI

Published by
Lotus Press Publishers & Distributors

Learn to
Speak and Write
HINDI

P.K. Agarwal
B.Com., M.A. (Hindi)
PGD in Translation
Sampadan Kala Visharad

Lotus PRESS

4735/22, Prakash Deep Building
Ansari Road, Darya Ganj,
New Delhi - 110002

Lotus Press : Publishers & Distributors
Unit No. 220, 2nd Floor, 4735/22, Prakash Deep Building,
Ansari Road, Darya Ganj, New Delhi- 110002
Ph.: 41325510, 98118-38000
• E-mail : lotuspress1984@gmail.com
www.lotuspress.co.in

Learn to Speak and Write Hindi
© **2023, P. K. Agarwal**
ISBN: 81-8382-062-X

Printed & Published by : **Lotus Press Publisher & Distributors**, New Delhi-02

Introduction To The Book

Our books on **LANGUAGES** have been designed keeping in mind the increasing numer of tourists, businessmen and others who visit these countries very often.

These books can also serve as a basis for a more complete study of these languages.

Learners who use these books can easily make themselves understood where these languages are spoken. By reading these books, one is not required to learn a long list of grammatical rules.

The vocabularies in these books have been carefully selected to give every learner the words that are needed in all aspects of everyday life.

We, at Lotus Press, are pretty confident that these books will give the learners as a useful introduction to these languagess they are spoken and written. This can eventually lead the learners to achieve a complete mastery on their chosen lanaguage.

LEARN TO SPEAK AND WRITE HINDI helps you to get acquainted with the Hindi language. This will surely enable you to speak and write Hindi as fluently just the way the typical Indians do. Happy learning...

-Publishers ◆

To My Learner Friends

First of all I welcome you and convey my sincere thanks to select this book for your Hindi learning. You are well aware that Hindi is not only the National Language of India but also the most-widely-spoken language in the country.

In this book, the main emphasis is given on the simple and easy conversation. Hence, a lot of words in daily use and a number of conversational exercises have been included for the purpose, which of course, will improve the vocabulary of the reader in a very simple and systematic manner.

I hope that this method will be very useful for the beginners. Efforts are made to cover all the relevant aspects as per your expectations. Moreover, a new part has also been included in this revised edition for the frequent use of tourists; particularly from abroad.

At the end, I convey my sincere thanks to my wife Smt. Saroj Agarwal, my son Animesh Aggarwal and my daughter Ms. Swarnima also for their remarkable co-operation in finalize and presenting the contents of this book in such a useful and balanced manner.

You will find this book as the simplest one to learn Hindi in your daily use. So enjoy a pleasant reading. Your valuable suggestions are always welcomed to make this book better and more useful.

All the best!

P.K. Agarwal
87, Tarun Vihar Apartments,
Sector 13, Rohini,
Delhi-110085.

CONTENTS

PART I : BASICS OF HINDI LANGUAGE

1. Alphabets and Pronunciation   11
   (Vowels, Consonants and Phonetics)
2. Combining Letters   16
3. Basic Grammar   18
4. Numbers and Numerals—   22
   I. Counting II. Ordinal Numbers
   III. Quantitative Numbers IV. Fractions

PART II : WORDS RELATED TO HUMANKIND

5. Animals / Animals in Water /Birds / Worms &
   Insects / Younglings of Animals   29
6. Cereals & Food Stuff / Flowers /
   Fruits and Dry fruits / Spices / Trees and its
   Contents / Vegetables   35
7. Personality / Professions &
   Occupations / Relations   42
8. Diseases & Physical Defects / Parts of
   Human Body   48

PART III : GENERAL WORDS IN DAILY LIFE

9. Dresses & Clothing/Metals & Stones/Ornaments,
   Make up & Jewels / World of Nature   55
10. Colours / Directions / Months / Planets/
    Seasons / Surroundings / Time denoting
    words / Weekdays   61
11. Building & its parts / Household
    Articles   67
12. Army and War / Items of Stationery /
    Musical Instruments / Tools   73

PART IV : GENERAL CONVERSATION

13. Common Sentences   80

14. Greetings / Invitation / Meeting and
    Parting / Gratitude / Congratulations
    and Good Wishes / Request /
    Permission / Instructions   87

15. Encouragement and Consent / Anger and
    Quarrel / Apologies / Time / Weather /
    Education / Health / Some Do's /
    Some Don'ts   96

16. Important Conversations—
    On arrival / Tourist office / Railway Station /
    Enquiry at Station / At Bus Stop / As Guest /
    At the Shop / With Taxi Driver / At a Hotel   107

PART V : MISCELLANEOUS EXPRESSIONS

17. Idioms and Phrases   122

18. Adjectives / Verbs in daily use / Genders   128

19. Similar Words having different meanings   136

20. Some more Expressions   146

PART VI : COMMON KEYWORDS FOR TOURISTS

21. Indian States and Capitals / Union Territories /
    Statewise Official Languages / 50 Big Cities of
    India   158

22. Famous Indian Tourist Spots: Places/
    Attraction/ Monuments/Hill Stations/
    Beaches/ Religious Sites   167

23. State and Regionwise Popular
    Foods, Dishes and Some Famous
    Indian Sweets   177

Chapter 1

Alphabets and Pronunciations

My Dear friend,

The Hindi is known as one of the most simple, beautiful and scientific language in the world. Its script is called **Devnagari**, which consists of 12 vowels and 36 consonants. Now join hands, come with me and read the following chart carefully:-

Vowels (स्वर)

a	aa	i	ee	u	oo
अ	आ	इ	ई	उ	ऊ
e	ai	o	au	an	ah
ए	ऐ	ओ	औ	अं	अः

Consonants (व्यंजन)

ka	kha	ga	gha	ng
क	ख	ग	घ	ङ
cha	chha	ja	jha	nya
च	छ	ज	झ	ञ
ta	tha	da	dha	na
ट	ठ	ड	ढ	ण
ta	tha	da	dha	na
त	थ	द	ध	न
pa	pha	ba	bha	ma
प	फ	ब	भ	म

Letters in bold have a hard sound

Other letters have a soft sound

ya	ra	la	va
य	र	ल	व

sha	sha	sa	ha
श	ष	स	ह

ksha	tra	gya
क्ष	त्र	ज्ञ

These 3 are **joint alphabets** (ka+sha, ta+ra, ja+na)

Notes:

1. Letters क, ख़, ग़, ज़, and फ़ have also been absorbed in Hindi from Urdu language and their corresponding phonetic sound in English is generally similar to **q, kha, gha, z** and **f/ph** respectively.

2. In Hindi, while pronounce consonants, these are compounding with vowels written alongwith them. Generally, the consonants include the short sound of vowel **A**. Like क has the sound of **K** and short **A**, whereas क् denotes **K** only. Some other examples are— **NA** represents न and **N** means न्; **DA** means द and **D** means द्. The sign ( ) below the consonants represents a half alphabet and is called a Halant sign in Hindi.

3. The alphabet ड़ would be written as **r/d** and ढ़ would be written as **rh/dh**.

4. ङ **NG** and ञ **NYA** are not written independently.

Phonetic form of Vowels and Consonants

As you know, the English alphabets are having various sounds, and hence no specific pronunciation can be given to them in general. With a view to understand them in connection with the Hindi alphabets, let us have a look on the following table:-

ध्वनि स्वर (Phonetics of Vowels)

वर्ण	ध्वनि	उदाहरण	हिंदी उच्चारण	अर्थ	रोमन लिपि में
Alphabet	Sound	Example	Pronunciation	Meaning	In Roman Script
A	ए	Gate	गेट	दरवाज़ा	*Darwaazaa*
		Late	लेट	देरी	*Deree*
	ऐ	Cat	कैट	बिल्ली	*Billee*
		Mat	मैट	चटाई	*Chataaee*
	अ	Ashok	अशोक	(पेड़ का नाम)	*(Name of a tree)*
		Anita	अनिता	(लड़की का नाम)	*(Name of a girl)*
	आ	Car	कार	कार	*Car*
		Far	फार	दूर	*Door*
		Jar	जार	मर्तबान	*Martbaan*
E	ऐ	Ever	ऐवर	हमेशा	*Hameshaa*
	ई	Ear	ईयर	कान	*Kaan*
	इ	Eleven	इलेवन	ग्यारह	*Gyaarah*
	आ	Eye	आई	आँख	*Aankh*
I	इ	It	इट	यह	*Yah*
	ई	Idiot	ईडियट	बेवकूफ़	*Bewakoof*
	आय	Iron	आयरन	लोहा	*Lohaa*
O	औ	Onkaar	औंकार	(ईश्वर का नाम)	*(Name of god)*
		Om	ओम	(एक मंत्र)	*(A Mantra)*

	आ	Owl	आउल	उल्लू	*Ulloo*
	अ	Son	सन	बेटा	*Betaa*
	ऑ	On	ऑन	पर	*Par*
U	अं	Cut	कट	काटना	*Kaatnaa*
	उ	Put	पुट	रखना	*Rakhnaa*
	ऊ	Rule	रूल	नियम	*Niyam*
	यू	Mule	म्यूल	खच्चर	*Khachchar*
		Unit	यूनिट	इकाई	*Ikaaee*

ध्वनि व्यंजन (Phonetics of Consonants)

B	ब	Bell	बैल	घंटी	*Ghantee*
C	स	Face	फेस	चेहरा	*Chehraa*
	क	Cat	कैट	बिल्ली	*Billee*
D	द	Devi	देवी	(देवी)	*(Godess)*
	ड	Dear	डियर	प्रिय	*Priya*
F	फ	Fat	फैट	मोटा	*Motaa*
G	ग	Gate	गेट	दरवाज़ा	*Darwazaa*
	ज	Gem	जैम	रत्न	*Ratna*
H	ह	Hat	हैट	टोप	*Topa*
J	ज	Jar	जार	मर्तबान (बर्तन)	*Martbaan (a pot)*
K	क	Kite	काइट	पतंग	*Patanga*
L	ल	Lap	लैप	गोद	*Goda*

M	म	My	माय	मेरा	*Meraa*
N	न	Neat	नीट	साफ़	*Saaf*
P	प	Pin	पिन	पिन	*Pin*
Q	क्यू	Quick	क्विक	तेज	*Tej*
R	र	Rat	रैट	चूहा	*Choohaa*
S	स	Seat	सीट	सीट	*Seat*
	ज	Is	इज़	है	*Hai*
T	ट	Tap	टैप	नल	*Nal*
	त	Taal	ताल	तालाब	*Taalaab*
V	व	Vase	वास	फूलदान	*Phooldaan*
W	व	Walk	वॉक	चलना	*Chalnaa*
X	एक्स	X-mas	क्रिसमस	(एक त्यौहार)	*A festival*
	क्स	Fox	फॉक्स	लोमड़ी	*Lomdee*
	ज	Xerox	ज़ेरॉक्स	फोटोकॉपी	*Photocopy*
Y	इ	System	सिस्टम	विधि	*Vidhi*
	ई	Year	ईयर	वर्ष/साल	*Varsh/Saal*
	य	You	यू	तुम	*Tum*
	आई	Try	ट्राई	प्रयास/कोशिश	*Prayaas/ Koshish*
Z	ज	Zoo	जू	चिड़ियाघर	*Chiriyaaghar*

It is very important for the readers to keep in mind the phonetic symbol and pronunciation of each and every alphabet, as it will help them in easy learning of Hindi.

❑❑❑

Chapter 2

Combining letters

So my dear friend, after going through the whole list of Hindi vowels and consonants, the next step is also very important in understanding the Hindi pronunciation and how to join a consonant with a vowel.

For this, here we take the first consonant 'क'(KA) and see how all the 12 vowels can be joined with it respectively to produce 12 different forms of 'क'(KA):

1.　　क्+अ　　=　　क　　As 'cu' in cut
　　　　(k+A　　=　　KA)

2.　　क्+आ　　=　　का　　As 'ka' in kamikaze
　　　　(k+AA　=　　KAA)

3.　　क्+इ　　=　　कि　　As 'ki' in kiss
　　　　(k+I　　=　　KI)

4.　　क्+ई　　=　　की　　As 'kee' in keen
　　　　(k+EE　=　　KEE)

5.　　क्+उ　　=　　कु　　As 'cu' in cuckoo
　　　　(k+U　　=　　KU)

6.　　क्+ऊ　　=　　कू　　As 'coo' in cool
　　　　(k+OO　=　　KOO)

7.　　क्+ए　　=　　के　　As 'ca' in cake
　　　　(k+E　　=　　KE)

| 8. | कृ+ऐ | = | कै | As 'ca' in California |
| | (k+AI | = | KAI) | |

| 9. | कृ+ओ | = | को | As 'coa' in Coal |
| | (k+O | = | KO) | |

| 10. | कृ+औ | = | कौ | As 'co' in copy |
| | (k+AU | = | KAU) | |

| 11. | कृ+अं | = | कं | As 'kan' in kangaroo |
| | (k+AN | = | KAN) | |

| 12. | कृ+अः | = | कः | As 'cah' in cahoots |
| | (k+A'H | = | KA'H) | |

We may likewise, combine all other consonants with vowels and get the correct pronunciation. Now we are well acquainted with all the alphabets, their respective pronunciations and how a vowel is joined with a consonant to form a word. The next step is **'formation of a Hindi sentence'** but before that a few small tips on basic grammar are essential.

❑❑❑

Chapter 3

Basic Grammar

Some Important rules to be remembered are:-

(1).   In English the VERB is placed immediately after the subject and the object, but in Hindi, the verb is usually placed at the end of the sentence and the rest every other word has its place in between the subject at one end and the verb on the other.

Example: a.   Ram went to hotel.
Ram hotel gayaa
(राम होटल गया).

b.   Anita is eating bread.
Anita rotee khaa rahee hai
(अनिता रोटी खा रही है).

(2).   As in English language, the verb in a Hindi sentence undergoes a number of changes according to the SUBJECT and the TENSE. In Hindi, the verb has to change according to two more factors:

I.   The NUMBER and the GENDER of the OBJECT of a TRANSITIVE verb; and

II.   The NUMBER and the GENDER of the SUBJECT in case of an INTRANSITIVE verb.

The reader is advised to use his/her INSTINCT also **alongwith the INTELLECT** to have a broader grasp of this oriental language.

(3). As in English, Hindi language has MAIN verbs and AUXILLIARY verbs. The MAIN verbs are of two types. One type consists of (as in English) a SINGLE WORD and in the first form, all ending with na (ना):-

सोना	=	*sonaa*	=	to sleep
जाना	=	*jaanaa*	=	to go
खाना	=	*khaanaa*	=	to eat
दौड़ना	=	*daudnaa*	=	to run
हँसना	=	*hansnaa*	=	to laugh

But the second type of Hindi verbs, consists of TWO WORDS, i.e., a MAIN word followed by an ACCESSORY one:-

To kill	=	*maar daalnaa*	=	मार डालना
To wait	=	*intezaar karnaa*	=	इंतज़ार करना
To bid	=	*daaon lagaanaa*	=	दांव लगाना
To look	=	*dikhaayee denaa*	=	दिखाई देना
To faint	=	*behosh honaa*	=	बेहोश होना

When these are used in sentences, only the ACCESSORY word undergoes changes according to the TENSE and the SUBJECT; the main word remains unchanged:-

To kill: maar daala - maar daale - maar daalegaa.
To faint: behosh ho gayaa - behosh ho gaye - behosh ho jaayegaa.

The auxilliary verbs are given systematically in the following table:

SUBJECT:	Ist Person Singular	Ist Person Plural	IInd Person	IIIrd Person Singular	IIIrd Person Plural
TENSE: 1. Present -	Hoon हूँ	Hain हैं	Ho हो	Hai है	Hain हैं
2. Past -	Tha/Thee था/थी (m/f)	The थे	The थे	Tha/Thee था/थी (m/f)	The/ Theen थे/थीं (m/f)
3. Future -	Ga/Gee गा/गी (m/f)	Ge गे	Ge गे	Ga/Gee गा/गी (m/f)	Ge/Gee गे/गी (m/f)

While going through the formation of sentences, you will gradually become familiar with the use of the above auxilliary verbs.

(4). There are only two genders in Hindi-MASCULINE (Pulling पुल्लिंग) and FAMININE (Striling स्त्रीलिंग). The Gender is either based on sex (in case of human beings and animals) or based on usage. There are no hard and fast rules. According to the general rule, all words ending with the vowel 'a' are masculine and those ending with the vowel 'i' are feminine. Words ending in a consonant may be masculine or feminine but there are many exceptions to the rule, which can be understand by usage.

(5.) You may also note that there are no definite or indefinite ARTICLES in Hindi as well as no SILENT letters are there.

(6.)　　In Hindi, an adverb precedes the verb or adjective it qualifies. Sometimes, an adverb is repeated to emphasize and also for effectiveness of speech.

जल्दी - जल्दी = fast　　　धीरे - धीरे = slowly

आप कहाँ-कहाँ जाएँगे?　　Which are the places you will go to?
(when more than one place is indicated)

❑❑❑

Chapter 4

Numbers and Numerals

Before reading the table given below, please note the numbers used in Hindi are similar to the numbers we are using in the English.

I. Counting (गिनती)

Number	Hindi No.	In English	In Hindi	Pronunciation
1	1	One	एक	Ek
2	2	Two	दो	Do
3	3	Three	तीन	Teen
4	4	Four	चार	Chaar
5	5	Five	पाँच	Paanch
6	6	Six	छः/छह	Chhah
7	7	Seven	सात	Saat
8	8	Eight	आठ	Aath
9	9	Nine	नौ	Nau
10	10	Ten	दस	Dus
11	11	Eleven	ग्यारह	Gyaarah
12	12	Twelve	बारह	Baarah
13	13	Thirteen	तेरह	Terah
14	14	Fourteen	चौदह	Choudah
15	15	Fifteen	पंद्रह	Pandrah
16	16	Sixteen	सोलह	Solah

17	17	Seventeen	सत्रह	Satrah
18	18	Eighteen	अठारह	Athaarah
19	19	Nineteen	उन्नीस	Unnees
20	20	Twenty	बीस	Bees
21	21	Twenty one	इक्कीस	Ekkees
22	22	Twenty two	बाईस	Baaees
23	23	Twenty three	तेईस	Teis
24	24	Twenty four	चौबीस	Chaubees
25	25	Twenty five	पच्चीस	Pachchees
26	26	Twenty six	छब्बीस	Chhabbees
27	27	Twenty seven	सत्ताईस	Sattaaees
28	28	Twenty eight	अठाईस	Athaaees
29	29	Twenty nine	उनतीस	Unatees
30	30	Thirty	तीस	Tees
31	31	Thirty one	इकतीस	Ekatees
32	32	Thirty two	बत्तीस	Battees
33	33	Thirty three	तेंतीस	Tentees
34	34	Thirty four	चौंतीस	Chauntees
35	35	Thirty five	पैंतीस	Paintees
36	36	Thirty six	छत्तीस	Chhattees
37	37	Thirty seven	सैंतीस	Saintees
38	38	Thirty eight	अड़तीस	Artees
39	39	Thirty nine	उनतालीस	Untaalees
40	40	Forty	चालीस	Chaalees
41	41	Forty one	इकतालीस	Ektaalees
42	42	Forty two	बयालीस	Byaalees
43	43	Forty three	तेंतालीस	Tentalees
44	44	Forty four	चौवालीस	Chauvalees

45	45	Forty five	पैंतालीस	*Paintaalees*
46	46	Forty six	छियालीस	*Chhiyaalees*
47	47	Forty seven	सैंतालीस	*Saintaalees*
48	48	Forty eight	अड़तालीस	*Artaalees*
49	49	Forty nine	उनचास	*Unchaas*
50	50	Fifty	पचास	*Pachaas*
51	51	Fifty one	इक्यावन	*Ikyaavan*
52	52	Fifty two	बावन	*Baavan*
53	53	Fifty three	तिरेपन	*Tirepan*
54	54	Fifty four	चौवन	*Chauvan*
55	55	Fifty five	पचपन	*Pachpan*
56	56	Fifty six	छप्पन	*Chhappan*
57	57	Fifty seven	सत्तावन	*Sattaavan*
58	58	Fifty eight	अठावन	*Athaavan*
59	59	Fifty nine	उनसठ	*Unsath*
60	60	Sixty	साठ	*Saath*
61	61	Sixty one	इकसठ	*Iksath*
62	62	Sixty two	बासठ	*Baasath*
63	63	Sixty three	तिरेसठ	*Tiresath*
64	64	Sixty four	चौंसठ	*Chaunsath*
65	65	Sixty five	पैंसठ	*Painsath*
66	66	Sixty six	छियासठ	*Chhiyaasath*
67	67	Sixty seven	सड़सठ	*Sarsath*
68	68	Sixty eight	अड़सठ	*Arsath*
69	69	Sixty nine	उनहत्तर	*Unhattar*
70	70	Seventy	सत्तर	*Sattar*
71	71	Seventy one	इकहत्तर	*Ikhattar*
72	72	Seventy two	बहत्तर	*Bahattar*

73	73	Seventy three	तिहत्तर	*Tihattar*
74	74	Seventy four	चौहत्तर	*Chauhattar*
75	75	Seventy five	पिचहत्तर	*Pichhattar*
76	76	Seventy six	छिहत्तर	*Chhihattar*
77	77	Seventy seven	सतहत्तर	*Satahattar*
78	78	Seventy eight	अठहत्तर	*Athhattar*
79	79	Seventy nine	उनासी	*Unaasee*
80	80	Eighty	अस्सी	*Assee*
81	81	Eighty one	इक्यासी	*Ikyasee*
82	82	Eighty two	बयासी	*Bayaasee*
83	83	Eighty three	तिरासी	*Tiraasee*
84	84	Eighty four	चौरासी	*Chauraasee*
85	85	Eighty five	पिचासी	*Pichaasee*
86	86	Eighty six	छियासी	*Chhiyaasee*
87	87	Eighty seven	सत्तासी	*Sattaasee*
88	88	Eighty eight	अठासी	*Athaasee*
89	89	Eighty nine	नवासी	*Navaasee*
90	90	Ninety	नब्बे	*Nabbe*
91	91	Ninety one	इक्यानवे	*Ikyaanve*
92	92	Ninety two	बानवे	*Baanve*
93	93	Ninety three	तिरानवे	*Tiraanve*
94	94	Ninety four	चौरावने	*Chauraanve*
95	95	Ninety five	पिचानवे	*Pichaanve*
96	96	Ninety six	छियावने	*Chhiyaanve*
97	97	Ninety seven	सत्तानवे	*Sattaanve*
98	98	Ninety eight	अठानवे	*Athaanve*
99	99	Ninety nine	निन्यानवे	*Ninyaanve*
100	100	Hundred	सौ	*Sau*

| 1000 | 1000 | Thousand | हज़ार | *Hazaar* |
| 100000 | 100000 | Lac | लाख | *Lakh* |

II. Ordinal Numbers (क्रमसूचक संख्याएं)

Number	*In English*	*In Hindi*	*Pronunciation*
1st	First	पहला	*Pahlaa*
2nd	Second	दूसरा	*Doosraa*
3rd	Third	तीसरा	*Teesraa*
4th	Fourth	चौथा	*Chauthaa*
5th	Fifth	पाँचवां	*Paanchvaan*
6th	Sixth	छठा	*Chhathaa*
7th	Seventh	सातवाँ	*Saatavaan*
8th	Eigth	आठवाँ	*Aathavaan*
9th	Ninth	नौंवा	*Nauvaan*
10th	Tenth	दसवाँ	*Dasavaan*
11th	Eleventh	ग्यारहवाँ	*Gyarahvaan*
12th	Twelfth	बारहवाँ	*Barahavaan*
13th	Thirteenth	तेरहवाँ	*Terahavaan*
14th	Fourteenth	चौदहवाँ	*Chaudahavaan*
15th	Fifteenth	पंद्रहवाँ	*Pandrahavaan*
16th	Sixteenth	सोलहवाँ	*Solahavaan*
17th	Seventeenth	सत्रहवाँ	*Satrahavaan*
18th	Eighteenth	अठारहवाँ	*Atharahavaan*
19th	Nineteenth	उन्नीसवाँ	*Unneesvaan*
20th	Twentieth	बीसवाँ	*Beesvaan*
30th	Thirtieth	तीसवाँ	*Teesvaan*
40th	Fortieth	चालीसवाँ	*Chaaleesvaan*
50th	Fiftieth	पचासवाँ	*Pachaasvaan*

60th	Sixtieth	साठवाँ	*Saathvaan*
70th	Seventieth	सत्तरवाँ	*Sattarvaan*
80th	Eightieth	अस्सीवाँ	*Asseevaan*
90th	Ninetieth	नब्बेवाँ	*Nabbevaan*
100th	Hundredth	सौवाँ	*Sauvaan*
1000th	Thousandth	हज़ारवाँ	*Hazaarvaan*

III. Quantitative Numbers (मात्रात्मक संख्याएं)

In English	*In Hindi*	*Pronunciation*
Double	दुगुना	*Dugunaa*
Triple	तिगुना	*Tigunaa*
Quadruple/Four fold	चौगुना	*Chaugunaa*

(Please add **'Fold'** with all other English numbers).

Once	एक बार	*ek baar*
Twice	दो बार	*do baar*
Thrice	तीन बार	*teen baar*
Four times	चार बार	*chaar baar*

(Please add **'Times'** with all other English numbers).

IV. Fractions of Number (अंक के भाग)

English	*Sign* चिन्ह		*Pronunciation*
1. Half	$\frac{1}{2}$	आधा	*Aadhaa*
2. One-third	$\frac{1}{3}$	तिहाई	*Tihaayee*
3. Quarter/One-fourth	$\frac{1}{4}$	चौथाई	*Chauthayee*

4. One and Quarter	$1\frac{1}{4}$	सवा	*Savaa*
5. One and half	$1\frac{1}{2}$	डेढ़	*Derha*
6. Two and a half	$2\frac{1}{2}$	ढाई	*Dhaayee*

Symbols of Calculation (गणना के चिन्ह)

English	Sign	चिन्ह	Pronunciation
1. To add	(+)	जमा करना	*Jamaa karnaa*
2. To divide	(÷)	भाग देना	*Bhaag dena*
3. To multiply	(×)	गुणा करना	*Gunaa karnaa*
4. To substract	(−)	घटाना	*Ghataanaa*

❏❏❏

Chapter 5

Animals / Water Animals /Birds / Worms & Insects /Younglings of Animals

Friends, you have understood the basic concept of the language formation in the Ist part of this book. Now, some words of daily use are given herebelow under various tables so that you may understand and learn them to make your communication simple and easily understandable:-

Name of Animals (जानवरों के नाम)

	English	हिंदी	Pronunciation
1.	Ape	लंगूर	*Langoor*
2.	Ass	गधा	*Gadhaa*
3.	Bear	भालू	*Bhaaloo*
4.	Bitch	कुतिया	*Kutiyaa*
5.	Bull	बैल / सांड	*Bail / Saand*
6.	Bison	भैंसा	*Bhensaa*
7.	Buffallo	भैंस	*Bhens*
8.	Bullock	बैल	*Bail*
9.	Camel	ऊँट	*Oont*
10.	Chamelion	गिरगिट	*Girgit*
11	Cow	गाय	*Gaai*
12.	Cat	बिल्ली	*Billee*
13.	Chimpangee	वनमानुष	*Vanmaanush*

14.	Dog	कुत्ता	*Kuttaa*
15.	Deer	हिरण	*Hiran*
16.	Elephant	हाथी	*Haathee*
17.	Fox	लोमड़ी	*Lomadee*
18.	Goat	बकरी	*Bakaree*
19.	Hare	खरगोश	*Kharagosh*
20.	Hind	बारहसिंगी	*Baarahsingee*
21.	Horse	घोड़ा	*Ghodaa*
22.	Hyean	लकड़बग्घा	*Lakarbagghaa*
23.	Jackel	गीदड़	*Geedar*
24.	Leopard	तेंदुआ	*Tenduaa*
25.	Lion	शेर	*Sher*
26.	Mare	घोड़ी	*Ghodee*
27.	Mongoose	नेवला	*Nevalaa*
28.	Monkey	बंदर	*Bandar*
29.	Mole	छछूंदर	*Chhachhundar*
30.	Mule	खच्चर	*Khachachar*
31.	Mouse	चूहा	*Choohaa*
32.	Pig	सूअर	*Sooar*
33.	Pony	टट्टू	*Tattoo*
34.	Porcupine	साही	*Saahee*
35.	Panther	चीता	*Cheetaa*
36.	Python	अजगर	*Ajgar*
37.	Rabbit	खरगोश	*Kharagosh*
38.	Rhinoceros	गैंडा	*Gendaa*
39.	Sheep	भेड़	*Bher*
40.	Squirrel	गिलहरी	*Gilaheree*
41.	Snake	साँप	*Saanp*
42.	Stag	बारहसिंगा	*Barahsingaa*
43.	Swine	सूअरी	*Sooaree*

44.	Tiger	बाघ	*Baagh*
45.	Tigress	बाघिन	*Baaghin*
46.	Wolf	भेड़िया	*Bheriyaa*
47.	Zebra	ज़ेबरा	*Zebra*

Animals in water (पानी के जीव)

English	*हिंदी*	*Pronunciation*
1. Crab	केकड़ा	*Kekraa*
2. Crocodile	मगरमच्छ	*Magharmachh*
3. Fish	मछली	*Machhlee*
4. Frog	मेंढ़क	*Maindhak*
5. Hippocampus	अश्वमीन	*Ashwameen*
6. Hippopotamus	दरियाई घोड़ा	*Dariaaee ghoraa*
7. Leech	जौंक	*Jaunk*
8. Tortoise	कछुआ	*Kachhuaa*

Name of Birds (पक्षियों के नाम)

English	*हिंदी*	*Pronunciation*
1. Bat	चमगादड़	*Chamgaadar*
2. Crow	कौआ	*Kauvaa*
3. Cock	मुर्गा	*Murgaa*
4. Crane	सारस	*Saaras*
5. Cuckoo	कोयल	*Koyal*
6. Dove	फाख्ता	*Phakhtaa*
7. Duck	बत्तख	*Battakh*
8. Goose	हंस/हंसिनी	*Hans/Hansini*

	English	हिंदी	Pronunciation
9.	Eagle	गरूड़	*Garuda*
10.	Hawk	बाज़	*Baaz*
11.	Hen	मुर्गी	*Murgee*
12.	Kite	चील	*Cheel*
13.	Magpie	नीलकंठ	*Neel kantha*
14.	Nightingale	बुलबुल	*Bulbul*
15.	Owl	उल्लू	*Ulloo*
16.	Parrot	तोता	*Totaa*
17.	Peacock	मोर	*Mora*
18.	Pigeon	कबूतर	*Kabootar*
19.	Peahen	मोरनी	*Moranee*
20.	Partiridge	तीतर	*Teetar*
21.	Quail	बटेर	*Bater*
22.	Sparrow	चिड़िया	*Chidiyaa*
23.	Swan	हंस	*Hans*
24.	Vulture	गिद्ध	*Giddha*
25.	Wood pecker	कठफोड़वा	*Kathforwaa*
26.	Weaver bird	बया	*Bayaa*

Worms & Insects (कीट ओर कीड़े)

	English	*हिंदी*	*Pronunciation*
1.	Ant	चींटी	*Cheentee*
2.	Bug	खटमल	*Khatmal*
3.	Butterfly	तितली	*Titalee*
4.	Fly	मक्खी	*Makkhee*
5.	Flea	पिस्सु	*Pissu*

6.	Glow worm	जुगनू	*Jugnoo*
7.	Grass hopper	टिड्डा	*Tiddaa*
8.	Honey Bee	शहद की मक्खी	*Shahad Kee Makkhee*
9.	Lizard	छिपकली	*Chhipkalee*
10.	Lice	जूँ	*Joon*
11.	Locust	टिड्डी	*Tiddee*
12.	Mosquito	मच्छर	*Machchhar*
13.	Scorpion	बिच्छू	*Bichchhoo*
14.	Spider	मकड़ी	*Makadee*
15.	Silk worm	रेशम का कीड़ा	*Resham Kaa Keeraa*
16.	Snail	घोंघा	*Ghonghaa*
17.	Tadpole	मेंढ़क का बच्चा	*Maindhak (Young one)*
18.	Wasp	ततैया	*Tataiyaa*

Younglings of Animals (जानवरों के बच्चों के नाम)

English	*हिंदी*	*Pronunciation*
1. Calf (of cow)	गाय का बच्चा	*Gaaya ka bachchaa*
2. Chicken (of hen)	मुर्गी का बच्चा	*Murgee ka bachchaa*
3. Colt (of horse)	घोड़े का बच्चा	*Ghode ka bachchaa*
4. Cub (of bear)	भालू का बच्चा	*Bhaaloo ka bachchaa*
5. Cub (of lion)	शेर का बच्चा	*Sher ka bachchaa*
6. Cub (of tiger)	बाघ का बच्चा	*Baagh ka bachchaa*
7. Cub (of wolf)	भेड़िये का बच्चा	*Bheriye ka bachchaa*
8. Cygnet (of swan)	हंस का बच्चा	*Hans ka bachchaa*

9. Foal (of ass)   गधे का बच्चा   *Ghadhe ka bachchaa*
10. Fawn (of deer)   हिरन का बच्चा   *Hiran ka bachchaa*
11. Kid (of goat)   बकरी का बच्चा   *Bakree ka bachchaa*
12. Kitten (of cat)   बिल्ली का बच्चा   *Billee ka bachchaa*
13. Lamb (of sheep)   भेड़ का बच्चा   *Bhed ka bachchaa*
14. Leveret (of hare) खरगोश का बच्चा   *Khargosh ka bachchaa*
15. Puppy (of dog)   कुत्ते का बच्चा   *Kutte ka bachchaa*
16. Tadpole (of frog) मेंढक का बच्चा   *Mendhak ka bachchaa*

❏❏❏

Chapter 6

Cereals & Food Stuff / Flowers / Fruits and Dry Fruits / Spices / Trees and its Contents / Vegetables

Cereals and Food Stuff (अनाज व खाद्य वस्तुएँ)

English	हिंदी	Pronunciation
1. Barley	जौ	*Jau*
2. Biscuit	बिस्कुट	*Biskut*
3. Bread	रोटी/चपाती	*Rotee/Chapaatee*
4. Butter	मक्खन	*Makkhan*
5. Chicken	मुर्गी का मांस	*Maans of hen*
6. Cereals	दाल	*Daal*
7. Coconut	नारियल	*Naariyal*
8. Cottage cheese	पनीर	*Paneer*
9. Curd	दही	*Dahee*
10. Dry fruit	मेवा	*Mevaa*
11. Egg	अण्डा	*Andaa*
12. Flour	आटा	*Aataa*
13 Gram	चना	*Chanaa*
14. Honey	शहद	*Shahad*
15. Jaggery	गुड़	*Gur*
16. Mash	दलिया	*Daliyaa*
17. Maize	मक्का	*Makkaa*
18. Millet	बाजरा	*Baajaraa*

19. Milk	दूध	*Doodh*
20. Mutton	भेड़ का माँस	*Maans (of sheep)*
21. Meat Flesh	माँस	*Maans*
22. Oil	तेल	*Tel*
23. Pickle	अचार	*Achaar*
24. Pork	सुअर का माँस	*Maans (of pig)*
25. Rice	चावल	*Chaaval*
26. Sugarcane	गन्ना	*Gannaa*
27. Sourmilk	छाछ	*Chhaachh*
28. Sweets	मिठाईयाँ	*Mithaaeean*
29. Sugar	चीनी	*Cheenee*
30. Tea	चाय	*Chaai*
31. Wheat	गेहूँ	*Gehoon*

Name of Flowers (फूलों के नाम)

English	*हिंदी*	*Pronunciation*
1. Balsam	गुलमेहंदी	*Gulmehandee*
2. Daisy	गुलबहार	*Gulbahaar*
3. Jasmine	चमेली	*Chamelee*
4. Lily	कुमुदिनी	*Kumudinee*
5. Lotus	कमल	*Kamal*
6. Magnolia	चम्पा	*Champaa*
7. Marigold	गेंदा	*Gendaa*
8. Rose	गुलाब	*Gulaab*
9. Sunflower	सूरजमुखी	*Soorajmukhee*
10. Touch me not	छुई-मुई	*Chhuee-muee*

Fruits and Dry Fruits (फलों/मेवों के नाम)

	English	हिंदी	Pronunciation
1.	Apple	सेब	*Seb*
2.	Apricot	खुबानी	*Khubaanee*
3.	Almond	बादाम	*Baadaam*
4.	Banana	केला	*Kelaa*
5.	Black berry	जामुन	*Jaamun*
6.	Cashewnut	काजू	*Kaajoo*
7.	Chestnut	अखरोट	*Akhrot*
8.	Coconut	नारियल	*Naariyal*
9.	Currant	किशमिश	*Kishmish*
10.	Custard apple	शरीफ़ा	*Shareephaa*
11.	Date	खजूर	*Khazoor*
12.	Fig	अंजीर	*Anjeer*
13.	Groundnut	मूँगफली	*Moongphalee*
14.	Grape	अंगूर	*Angoor*
15.	Guava	अमरूद	*Amrood*
16.	Jackfruit	कटहल	*Kathal*
17.	Mango	आम	*Aam*
18.	Mulberry	शहतूत	*Shahtoot*
19.	Melon	खरबूज़ा	*Kharboozaa*
20.	Orange	संतरा	*Santaraa*
21.	Papaya	पपीता	*Papeetaa*
22.	Pear	नाशपाती	*Nashpaatee*
23.	Peach	आड़ू	*Aadoo*
24.	Plum	आलू बुखारा	*Aaloobukhaaraa*
25.	Pineapple	अनानास	*Annanaas*
26.	Pomegranate	अनार	*Anaar*
27.	Raisin	मुनक्का	*Munakkaa*
28.	Watermelon	तरबूज़	*Tarbooz*

Name of Spices (मसालों के नाम)

English	हिंदी	Pronunciation
1. Aniseed	सौंफ	*Saunph*
2. Asafoetida	हींग	*Heenga*
3. Black pepper	काली मिर्च	*Kaalee Mirch*
4. Bayleaf	तेजपत्ता	*Tejpatta*
5. Cardamom	इलायची	*Ilaayachee*
6. Chilly	लाल मिर्च	*Laal Mirch*
7. Cinnamon	दाल चीनी	*Dall Cheenee*
8. Cloves	लौंग	*Launga*
9. Coriander	धनिया	*Dhaniyaa*
10. Cuminseed	जीरा	*Jeeraa*
11. Dry ginger	सौंठ	*Sauntha*
12. Fenugreek	मेथी	*Methee*
13. King's cumin	अजवायन	*Ajvaayan*
14. Mace	जावित्री	*Jaavitree*
15. Mustard	राई⁄सरसों	*Raaee/Sarson*
16. Nutmeg	जायफल	*Jaayafal*
17. Saffron	केसर	*Kesar*
18. Salt	नमक	*Namak*
19. Sesame	तिल	*Til*
20. Tamarind	इमली	*Imlee*
21. Turmeric	हल्दी	*Haldee*

Trees & its Contents (पेड़ और उसके भाग)

	English	हिंदी	Pronunciation
1.	Acacia	बबूल	*Babul*
2.	Bamboo	बांस	*Baans*
3.	Banyan	बरगद	*Baragad*
4.	Branch	टहनी/शाखा	*Tehaneel Shaakhaa*
5.	bud	कली	*Kalee*
6.	Bark	छाल	*Chhaal*
7.	Cane	बेंत/गन्ना	*Bent/gannaa*
8.	Ceddar	देवदार	*Devadaar*
9.	Flower	फूल	*Phool*
10.	Fibre	रेशा	*Reshaa*
11.	Germ	अंकुर	*Ankur*
12.	Graft	कलम	*Kalam*
13.	Gum	गोंद	*Gonda*
14.	Grass	घास	*Ghaas*
15.	Indigo	नील	*Neel*
16.	Juice	रस	*Rasa*
17.	Leaf	पत्ता	*Pattaa*
18.	Margosa	नीम	*Neem*
19.	Oak	बलूत	*Baloot*
20.	Pine	चीड़	*Cheera*
21.	Pulp	गूदा	*Goodaa*
22.	Root	जड़	*Jara*
23.	Rind	छाल	*Chhaal*

24. Stem	तना	*Tanaa*
25. Seed	बीज	*Beej*
26. Skin	छिलका	*Chhilkaa*
27. Teak	सागवान	*Saagvaan*
28. Tamarind	इमली	*Imlee*
29. Tobbacco	तम्बाकू	*Tambaakoo*
30. Thorn	कांटा	*Kaantaa*

Name of Vegetables (सब्जियों के नाम)

English	*हिंदी*	*Pronunciation*
1. Arum	अरबी	*Arbee*
2. Bean	सेम	*Sem*
3. Brinjal	बैंगन	*Baingan*
4. Cabbage	बन्दगोभी	*Banda gobhee*
5. Carrot	गाज़र	*Gaazar*
6. Chilly (Green)	हरी मिर्च	*Haree Mirch*
7. Coriander (green)	हरा धनिया	*Haraa Dhaniyaa*
8. Cauliflower	फूलगोभी	*Phool gobhee*
9. Cucumber	खीरा	*Kheeraa*
10. Garlic	लहसुन	*Lehsun*
11. Ginger	अदरक	*Adrak*
12. Gourd bottle	घीया	*Gheeyaa*
13. Lemon	नींबू	*Neemboo*
14. Lady finger	भिन्डी	*Bhindee*
15. Mint	पुदीना	*Pudeenaa*
16. Onion	प्याज़	*Pyaaz*
17. Peas	मटर	*Matar*

18. Potato	आलू	*Aaloo*
19. Pumpkin	कद्दू	*Kaddoo*
20. Radish	मूली	*Moolee*
21. Spinach	पालक	*Paalak*
22. Sweat potato	शकरकन्दी	*Shakarkandee*
23. Tomato	टमाटर	*Tamaatar*
24. Turnip	शलगम	*Shalgam*
25. Yam	कचालू	*Kachaaloo*

❑❑❑

Chapter 7

Personality / Professions & Occupations / Relations

About Personality (व्यक्तित्व संबंधी)

English	हिंदी	Pronunciation
1. Diffident	शंकालु	*Shankaaloo*
2. Egoist	अहंकारी	*Ahankaaree*
3. Extrovert	बर्हिमुखी	*Bahirmukhee*
4. Fatalist	भाग्यवादी	*Bhaagyavaadee*
5. Greedy	लालची	*Laalachee*
6. Illiterate	अशिक्षित/निरक्षर	*Ashikshit/*
7. Introvert	अन्तर्मुखी	*Antrarmukhee*
8. Incredible	अतुलनीय	*Atulneeya*
9. Notorious	कुख्यात	*Kukhyaat*
10. Optimist	आशावादी	*Aashaavaadee*
11. Pessimist	निराशावादी	*Niraashaavadee*
12. Religious	धार्मिक	*Dhaarmik*
		Nirakshar
13. Sadistic	परपीड़क	*Parapeedak*
14. Sophisticated	सुविज्ञ/विवेकी	*Suvigya/vivekee*
15. Talkative	बातूनी	*Baatoonee*
16. Vegeterian	शाकाहारी	*Shakahaaree*
17. Vaunter	शेखीबाज़	*Shekheebaaz*

Professions and Occupations (पेशा और व्यवसाय)

	English	हिंदी	Pronunciation
1.	Actor	अभिनेता	*Abhinetaa*
2.	Artist	कलाकार	*Kalaakaar*
3.	Author	लेखक	*Lekhak*
4.	Accountant	मुनीम/लेखाकार	*Muneem/ Lekhaakaar*
5.	Advocate	वकील	*Vakeel*
6.	Blacksmith	लुहार	*Luhaar*
7.	Barber	नाई	*Naayee*
8.	Broker	दलाल	*Dalaal*
9.	Book-binder	ज़िल्दसाज़	*Zildasaaz*
10.	Butcher	कसाई	*Kasaayee*
11.	Brazier	ठठेरा	*Thatheraa*
12.	Begger	भिखारी	*Bhikharee*
13.	Butler	भण्डारी	*Bhandaaree*
14.	Carpenter	बढ़ई	*Barhayee*
15.	Chemist	कैमिस्ट	*Chemist*
16.	Clerk	क्लर्क/लिपिक	*Clerk/lipik*
17.	Cook/Chef	रसोइया/बावर्ची	*Rasoiyaa/ Bawarchee*
18.	Confectioner	हलवाई	*Halvaayee*
19.	Coolie	कुली	*Kulee*
20.	Coachman	कोचवान	*Coachvaan*
21.	Contractor	ठेकेदार	*Thakedaar*
22.	Cashier	रोकड़िया	*Rokariyaa*
23.	Cobbler	मोची	*Mochee*
24.	Compounder	कम्पाउन्डर	*Compounder*

25.	Compositer	सम्मिश्रक	*Sammishrak*
26.	Copywriter	विज्ञापनकार	*Vigyaapankaar*
27.	Carrier	संवाहक	*Samvaahak*
28.	Cleaner	साफ करने वाला	*Saaf karne waalaa*
29.	Conductor	परिचालक	*Parichaalak*
30.	Constable	पुलिस का सिपाही	*Police kaa sipaahee*
31.	Chauffeur	कार चालक	*Car Chaalak*
32.	Druggist	दवा विक्रेता	*Davaa Vikretaa*
33.	Doctor	डॉक्टर/चिकित्सक	*Doctor/Chikitsak*
34.	Drummer	तबलची	*Tabalchee*
35.	Dentist	दन्त चिकित्सक	*Dant Chikitsak*
36.	Draftsman	मानचित्रक/प्रारूपकार	*Maanchitrak/ Praroopkaar*
37.	Dancer	नर्तक	*Nartak*
38.	Dramatist	नाटककार	*Naatakkaar*
39.	Dyer	रंगरेज़	*Rangrez*
40.	Editor	सम्पादक	*Sampaadak*
41.	Engineer	अभियन्ता	*Abhiyantaa*
42.	Examiner	परीक्षक	*Pareekshak*
43.	Enameller	मीनाकार	*Meenaakaar*
44.	Farmer	किसान	*Kisaan*
45.	Fisherman	मछुआरा	*Machhuaaraa*
46.	Gardener	माली	*Maalee*
47.	Goldsmith	सुनार	*Sunaar*
48.	Groom	दूल्हा	*Doolha*
49.	Hawker	फेरी वाला	*Feree vaalaa*
50.	Inspector	निरीक्षक	*Nireekshak*
51.	Inkman	रोशनाई करने वाला	*Roshnaaee karne waalaa*

52.	Jeweller	जौहरी	*Jauhari*
53.	Manager	प्रबन्धक	*Prabandhak*
54.	Milkman	ग्वाला/दूधिया	*Gwaalaa/ Doodhiyaa*
55.	Milkmaid	ग्वालन	*Gwaalan*
56.	Messanger	दूत	*Doot*
57.	Musician	संगीतकार	*Sangeetkaar*
58.	Magician	जादूगर	*Jaadoogar*
59.	Mechanic	मिस्त्री	*Mistree*
60.	Novelist	उपन्यास लेखक	*Upanyaas Lekhak*
61.	Nurse	नर्स/परिचारिका	*Nurse/ Parichaarikaa*
62.	Operator	चलाने वाला	*Chalaane waalaa*
63.	Potter	कुम्हार	*Kumhaar*
64.	Parcher	भड़भूजा	*Bharbhoojaa*
65.	Printer	मुद्रक	*Mudrak*
66.	Publisher	प्रकाशक	*Prakaashak*
67.	Poet	कवि	*Kavi*
68.	Peon	चपरासी	*Chaparaasee*
69.	Postman	डाकिया	*Daakiyaa*
70.	Priest	पुरोहित/पुजारी	*Purohit/Pujaaree*
71.	Painter	रंगसाज़	*Rangsaaz*
72.	Politician	राजनीतिज्ञ	*Raajneetigya*
73.	Proprietor	मालिक	*Maalik*
74.	Photographer	फोटो खींचने वाला	*Photo kheenchane waalaa*
75.	Sailor	नाविक	*Naavik*
76.	Shopkeeper	दुकानदार	*Dukaandaar*

77.	Sweeper	सफाई वाला	*Safaaee waalaa*
78.	Scavanger	झाड़ू वाला	*Jhaaroo waalaa*
79.	Surgeon	सर्जन/शल्य चिकित्सक	*Surgeon/Shalya chikitsak*
80.	Shoe-maker	जूता बनाने वाला	*Jootaa banaane waalaa*
81.	Sanitary Inspector	सफाई निरीक्षक	*Safaaee Nireekshak*
82.	Sculptor	मूर्तिकार	*Moortikaar*
83.	Tailor	दर्जी	*Darjee*
84.	Teacher	शिक्षक/अध्यापक	*Shikshak/ Adhyaapak*
85.	Treasurer	खजांची	*Khajaanchee*
86.	Turner	खरादने वाला	*Kharaadne waalaa*
87.	Writer	लेखक	*Lekhak*
88.	Washerman	धोबी	*Dhobee*
89.	Weaver	जुलाहा	*Julaahaa*
90.	Waiter	वेटर	*Waiter*
91.	Writer	लेखक	*Lekhak*

Name of Relations (रिश्तों के नाम)

English	*हिंदी*	*Pronunciation*
1. Aunt	चाची/मामी	*Chaachee*
2. Brother	भाई	*Bhaaee*
3. Brother-in-law	साला/जीजा	*Saalaa/Jeejaa*
4. Cousin	चचेराभाई/बहन	*Chachera bhaaee/bahan*
5. Customer	ग्राहक	*Graahak*

6.	Daughter	बेटी	*Betee*
7.	Daughter-in-law	बहु	*Bahu*
8.	Father	पिता	*Pitaa*
9.	Father-in-law	ससुर	*Sasur*
10.	Friend	दोस्त/मित्र	*Dost/mitra*
11.	Grand Father	दादा	*Daadaa*
12.	Grand Mother	दादी	*Daadee*
13.	Grand Daughter	पोती	*Potee*
14.	Grand Son	पोता	*Potaa*
15.	Guest	अतिथि/मेहमान	*Atithi/mehmaan*
16.	Heir	वारिस	*Vaaris*
17.	Husband	पति	*Pati*
18.	Landlord	जमींदार/मकान मालिक	*Zameendaar/ makaan maalik*
19.	Mother	माँ	*Maan*
20.	Mother-in-law	सास	*Saas*
21.	Maternal uncle	मामा	*Maamaa*
22.	Maternal aunt	मामी	*Maamee*
23.	Nephew	भतीजा/भान्जा	*Bhateeja/Bhaanjaa*
24.	Niece	भतीजी/भान्जी	*Bhateejee/Bhaanjee*
25.	Pupil	छात्र	*Chhaatra*
26.	Son	बेटा	*Betaa*
27.	Son-in-law	दामाद	*Daamaad*
28.	Sister	बहन	*Bahan*
29.	Step Father	सौतेला पिता	*Sautela Pitaa*
30.	Step Mother	सौतेली माँ	*Sautelee Maan*
31.	Step Brother	सौतेला भाई	*Sautelaa Bhaaee*
32.	Step Sister	सौतेली बहन	*Sautelee Bahan*
33.	Teacher	गुरु/शिक्षक	*Guru/Shikshak*
34.	Wife	पत्नी	*Patnee*

❏❏❏

Chapter 8

Diseases & Physical Defects / Parts of Human Body

Diseases & Physical defects (बीमारियाँ व शारीरिक दोष)

	English	हिंदी	Pronunciation
1.	Acidity	अम्ल पित्त	*Amla Pitta*
2.	Acne	मुँहासे	*Munhaase*
3.	Ailment	रोग/बीमारी	*Roga/Beemaaree*
4.	Anaemia	खून की कमी/ रक्तक्षीणता	*Khoon kee kamee/ Raktaksheentaa*
5.	Abortion	गर्भपात	*Garbhapaata*
6.	Asthma	दमा	*Damaa*
7.	Baldness	गंजापन	*Ganjaapan*
8.	Bleeding	खून बहना/ रक्तस्राव	*Khoon behnaa/ Raktasraava*
9.	Belching	डकार	*Dakaar*
10.	Bile	पित्त	*Pitta*
11.	Blindness	अंधापन	*Andhaapan*
12.	Breath	सांस	*Saans*
13.	Boil	फोड़ा	*Phodaa*
14.	Bronchitis	सांस की बीमारी	*Saans kee beemaaree*
15.	Cataract	मोतियाबिंद	*Motiyaabind*
16.	Cholera	हैज़ा	*Haizaa*

	English	Hindi	Transliteration
17.	Conjunctivities	आँख आना	*Aankh aanaa*
18.	Constipation	कब्ज़	*Kabza*
19.	Diorrhoea	अतिसार	*Atisaar*
20.	Dumbness	गूंगापन	*Goongaapan*
21.	Dysentry	पेचिश/दस्त	*Pachish/Dast*
22.	Dwarfness	बौनापन	*Baunaapan*
23.	Dropsy	जलोदर	*Jalodar*
24.	Eczeme	त्वचा की बीमारी	*Twachaa kee bimaaree*
25.	Epilepsy	मिरगी	*Miragee*
26.	Fever	बुखार	*Bukhaar*
27.	Fistula	भगन्दर	*Bhagandar*
28.	Fart	पाद	*Paad*
29.	Giddiness	चक्कर आना	*Chakkar aanaa*
30.	Griping	मरोड़	*Maroda*
31.	Health	स्वास्थ्य	*Swasthya*
32.	Heart attack	दिल का दौरा	*Dil kaa dauraa*
33.	Hernia	हर्निया	*Hernia*
34.	Hiccup	हिचकी	*Hichaki*
35.	Hunger	भूख	*Bhookh*
36.	Hunch backed	कुबड़ा	*Kubaraa*
37.	Hurt	चोट	*Chot*
38.	Indigestion	अपच	*Apach*
39.	Insomnia	अनिद्रा	*Anidraa*
40.	Itch	खुजली	*Khujlee*
41.	Jaundice	पीलिया	*Peeliyaa*
42.	Leprosy	कोढ़	*Korha*
43.	Lean	दुबला	*Dublaa*
44.	Lame	लंगड़ा	*Langaraa*
45.	Madness	पागलपन	*Paagalpan*

46.	Mole	मस्सा	*Massaa*
47.	Old age	बुढ़ापा	*Budhapaa*
48.	One eyed	काना	*Kaanaa*
49.	Pain	दर्द	*Dard*
50.	Paralysis	लकवा	*Lakvaa*
51.	Piles	बवासीर	*Bavaseer*
52.	Pimple	फुंसी	*Phunsee*
53.	Phlegm	कफ/बलगम	*Kaf/Balgam*
54.	Phobia	डर/भय	*Dar/Bhaya*
55.	Pus	मवाद/पीप	*Mavaad/Peep*
56.	Rheumatism	गठिया	*Gathiyaa*
57.	Ring worm	दाद	*Daad*
58.	Saliva	लार	*Laar*
59.	Sleep	नींद/निद्रा	*Neend/Nidraa*
60.	Sneezing	छींकना	*Chheenkanaa*
61.	Stone	पथरी	*Pathree*
62.	Stool	मल/पखाना	*Mal/Pakhaanaa*
63.	Sunstroke	लू लगना	*Loo laganaa*
64.	Sweat	पसीना	*Paseenaa*
65.	Swelling	सूजन	*Soojana*
66.	Sprain	मोच	*Mocha*
67.	Stomachache	पेट का दर्द	*Pet kaa dard*
68.	Short sight	अल्पदृष्टि	*Alpadrishti*
69.	Scabies	खुजली	*Khujlee*
70.	Spittle	थूक	*Thook*
71.	Tears	आंसू	*Aansoo*
72.	Typhus	काला ज्वर	*Kaalaa jwar*
73.	Tonsils	टॉन्सिल्स	*Tonsils*
74.	Tumour	गाँठ	*Gaanth*
75.	Typhoid	आंत्रज्वर	*Antrajwar*

76.	Tuberculosis	क्षय रोग/तपेदिक	*Kshayaroga/ Tapedic*
77.	Urine	मूत्र/पेशाब	*Mootra/Peshaab*
78.	Vomiting	उल्टी/कै	*Ulti/Kai*
79.	Voice	आवाज़	*Aawaaz*
80.	Wound	घाव	*Ghaav*
81.	Yawn	उबासी	*Ubaasee*

Parts of Human Body (मानव शरीर के अंग)

	English	*हिंदी*	*Pronunciation*
1.	Ankle	टखना	*Takhanaa*
2.	Arm	बाजू	*Baajoo*
3.	Armpit	बगल	*Bagal*
4.	Back	पीठ/कमर	*Peeth/Kamar*
5.	Back-bone	रीढ़ की हड्डी	*Reedh Kee Haddee*
6.	Beard	दाढ़ी	*Daadhee*
7.	Belly	पेट	*Peta*
8.	Blood	रक्त/खून	*Rakta/Khoon*
9.	Brain	दिमाग	*Dimaag*
10.	Breast	छाती (स्त्री)	*Chhaatee (female)*
11.	Bone	हड्डी	*Haddee*
12.	Calf	पिण्डली	*Pindalee*
13.	Chest	छाती (पुरुष)	*Chhaatee (Male)*
14.	Cheeks	गाल	*Gaal*
15.	Chin	ठोडी	*Thodee*
16.	Collar-bone	हंसुली की हड्डी	*Hansulee Kee Haddee*
17.	Ear	कान	*Kaan*
18.	Ear-drum	कर्णपटल	*Karnapatal*

19.	Elbow	कोहनी	*Kohanee*
20.	Eye	आँख	*Aankh*
21.	Eye-ball	आँख की पुतली	*Aankh Kee Putlee*
22.	Eye-brow	भौंह	*Bhonha*
23.	Eye-lid	पलक	*Palak*
24.	Eye-lash	बरौनी	*Baraunee*
25.	Face	चेहरा	*Cheharaa*
26.	Finger	अँगुली	*Angulee*
27.	Fist	मुट्ठी	*Mutthee*
28.	Foot	पैर	*Pair*
29.	Forehead	माथा	*Maathaa*
30.	Hand	हाथ	*Haath*
31.	Hair	बाल	*Baal*
32.	Head	सिर/सर	*Sir/Sar*
33.	Heart	दिल	*Dil*
34.	Heel	एड़ी	*Eidee*
35.	Hip	कूल्हा	*Koolhaa*
36.	Gullet	हलक	*Halak*
37.	Gum	मसूड़ा	*Massoraa*
38.	Jaw	जबड़ा	*Jabaraa*
39.	Joint	जोड़	*Jora*
40.	Knee	घुटना	*Ghutanaa*
41.	Kidney	गुर्दा	*Gurdaa*
42.	Lap	गोद	*Goda*
43.	Leg	टांग	*Taang*
44.	Liver	जिगर	*Jigar*
45.	Lip	होंठ	*Hontha*
46.	Lung	फेफड़ा	*Phephdaa*
47.	Mole	तिल/मस्सा	*Til/Massaa*

48.	Mouth	मुँह	*Munh*
49.	Moustache	मूँछ	*Moonchh*
50.	Mind	दिमाग	*Dimaag*
51.	Muscle	पेशी	*Peshee*
52.	Nail	नाखून	*Naakhoon*
53.	Neck	गर्दन/गला	*Gardan/Galaa*
54.	Nose	नाक	*Naak*
55.	Navel	नाभि	*Naabhi*
56.	Nerve	रग	*Rag*
57.	Nipple	चुचुक	*Chuchuk*
58.	Nostrill	नथुना	*Nathunaa*
59.	Palm	हथेली	*Hathelee*
60.	Palate	तालू	*Taloo*
61.	Pulse	नाड़ी	*Naaree*
62.	Penis	लिंग(शिश्न)	*Ling (Shishan)*
63.	Shoulder	कंधा	*Kandhaa*
64.	Skin	त्वचा/खाल	*Twachaa/Khaal*
65.	Skull	खोपड़ी	*Khoparee*
66.	Spine	रीढ़	*Reedha*
67.	Sole	तलवा	*Talwaa*
68.	Stomach	पेट	*Peta*
69.	Spleen	तिल्ली	*Tillee*
70.	Rib	पसली	*Paslee*
71.	Saliva	लार	*Laar*
72.	Rump	चूतड़/नितम्ब	*Chootar/Nitamb*
73.	Teat	स्तन/स्तनाग्र	*Stan/Stanaagra*
74.	Temple	कनपटी	*Kanapatee*
75.	Thigh	जाँघ	*Jaangh*
76.	Throat	गला	*Galaa*
77.	Thumb	अँगूठा	*Angootha*

78.	Toe	पांव की अंगुली	*Angulee (of Foot)*
79.	Tongue	जीभ	*Jeebh*
80.	Tooth	दाँत	*Daant*
81.	Vein	नस	*Nas*
82.	Vagina	योनि	*Yonee*
83.	Waist	कमर	*Kamar*
84.	Wrist	कलाई	*Kalaaee*
85.	Womb/Uterus	गर्भाशय/बच्चादानी	*Garbhaashaya/Bachchadaanee*
86.	Urinary bladder	मूत्राशय	*Mootraashaya*
87.	Trachea	सांस नली	*Saans nalee*

❑❑❑

Chapter 9

Dresses & Clothings / Metals & Stones / Ornaments, Make up & Jewels / World of Nature

Dresses & Clothings (पोशाकें और कपड़े)

English	हिंदी	Pronunciation
1. Blanket	कम्बल	*Kambal*
2. Bed-Sheet	चादर	*Chaadar*
3. Belt	पेटी	*Petee*
4. Blouse	ब्लाऊज	*Blouse*
5. Bra/Bodice	अंगिया/चोली	*Angiyaa/Cholee*
6. Brief	कच्छा/चड्डी	*Kachchhaa/Chaddhee*
7. Boot	जूता	*Joota*
8. Cap	टोपी	*Topee*
9. Coat	कोट	*Kot*
10. Cotton	सूत	*Soot*
11. Cloth	कपड़ा	*Kapadaa*
12. Frock	फ्रॉक	*Frock*
13. Gloves	दस्ताने	*Dastaane*
14. Hat	टोप	*Tope*
15. Hankerchief	रूमाल	*Rumaal*
16. Half-pant	निक्कर	*Nikkar*

18.	Laces	फीते	*Pheete*
19.	Muffler	मफलर	*Muffler*
20.	Napkin	नैपकिन	*Napkin*
21.	Nack-tie	गले की टाई	*Gale Kee Tie*
22.	Pants	पतलून	*Pataloon*
23.	Petticoat	पेटीकोट	*Peteecoat*
24.	Pocket	जेब	*Zeb*
25.	Quilt	रज़ाई	*Razaaee*
26.	Shirt	कमीज़	*Kameez*
27.	Sweater	स्वेटर	*Sweater*
28.	Shorts	निक्कर	*Nikkar*
29.	Socks	जुराब/मोजा	*Juraab/Mojaa*
30.	Stockings	बड़ी जुराबें	*Badee Juraabain*
31.	Saree	साड़ी	*Saree*
32.	Shoes	जूते	*Joote*
33.	Shawl	शॉल/दुशाला	*Shawl/Dushaalaa*
34.	Sleeve	आस्तीन	*Aasteen*
35.	Suit	सूट	*Suit*
36.	Silk	रेशम	*Resham*
37.	Towel	तौलिया	*Tauliyaa*
38.	Trousers	पतलून	*Pataloon*
39.	Turban	पगड़ी/साफा	*Pagree/Saafaa*
40.	Uniform	वर्दी	*Vardee*
41.	Underwear	कच्छा/जांघिया	*Kachchhaa/ Jaanghiyaa*
42.	Velvet	मखमल	*Makhmal*
43.	Veil	दुपट्टा/ओढ़नी/ चुनरी/चुन्नी	*Dupattaa/Orhanee Chunaree / Chunnee*
44.	Vest	बनियान	*Baniyaan*
45.	Wool	ऊन	*Oon*
46.	Yarn	सूत/धागा	*Soot/Dhaagaa*

Names of Metals & Stones (धातुओं व पत्थरों के नाम)

	English	हिंदी	Pronunciation
1.	Aluminium	एल्युमिनियम	*Aluminium*
2.	Brass	पीतल	*Peetal*
3.	Bronze	कांसा	*Kaansa*
4.	Coppper	तांबा	*Taambaa*
5.	Coal	कोयला	*Koyalaa*
6.	Charcoal	लकड़ी का कोयला	*Lakaree ka Koyalaa*
7.	Chalk	खड़िया	*Khariyaa*
8.	Gold	सोना	*Sonaa*
9.	Iron	लोहा	*Lohaa*
10.	Lead	सीसा	*Seesaa*
11.	Mica	अभ्रक	*Abharak*
12.	Mineral	खनिज	*Khanij*
13.	Mercury	पारा	*Paaraa*
14.	Marbel	संगमरमर	*Sangamarmar*
15.	Mine	खान	*Khaan*
16.	Ochre	गेरू	*Geroo*
17.	Platinum	प्लेटिनम	*Platinum*
18.	Radium	रेडियम	*Radium*
19.	Rock	चट्टान	*Chattaan*
20.	Sulphur	गन्धक	*Gandhak*
21.	Silver	चांदी	*Chaandee*
22.	Steel	स्टील	*Steel*
23.	Tin	टिन	*Tin*
24.	Zinc	जस्ता	*Jastaa*

Ornaments, Make up and Jewels
(आभूषण, प्रसाधन व रत्न)

English	हिंदी	Pronunciation
1. Anklet	पाज़ेब	Paazeb
2. Armpet	बाजूबंद	Baajooband
3. Bangles	चूड़ियाँ	Choodiyaan
4. Bracelet	कंगन	Kangan
5. Brooch	पिन	Pin
6. Clip	चिमटी	Chimatee
7. Coral	मूँगा	Moongaa
8. Chain	चेन	Chain
9. Chignon	जूड़ा	Joodaa
10. Collyrium	काजल	Kaajal
11. Cat's eye	लहसुनिया	Lehsuniyaa
12. Cream	क्रीम	Cream
13. Diamond	हीरा	Heeraa
14. Emerald	पन्ना	Pannaa
15. Ear-ring	कर्णफूल/बुंदा	Karnaphool/Bundaa
16. Ear-Stud	कान का गहना	Kaan Kaa Gehnaa
17. Gems	जवाहरात	Jawaaharaat
18. Hairpin	बालों की पिन	Baalon Kee Pin
19. Head Locket	माँग का टीका	Maang kaa Teekaa
20. Lipstic	लिपस्टिक	Lipstic
21. Mehandee	मेहंदी	Mehandee
22. Necklace	गले का हार	Gale Kaa Haar
23. Nose-Pin	नाक की पिन	Naak Kee Pin

24.	Nose-ring	नथनी/लौंग	*Nathanee/Laung*
25.	Pebble	बिल्लौर	*Billore*
26.	Powder	पाउडर	*Powder*
27.	Pearl	मोती	*Motee*
28.	Ring	अँगूठी	*Angoothi*
29.	Ruby	माणिक्य	*Manikya*
30.	Scent/Perfume	इत्र	*Itra*
31.	Shampoo	शैम्पू	*Shampoo*
32.	Sapphire	नीलम	*Neelam*
33.	Topaz	पुखराज	*Pukharaaj*
34.	Turquoise	फ़ीरोज़ा	*Feerozaa*
35.	Wrist watch	कलाई घड़ी	*Kalaaee Gharee*
36.	Wreath	माला	*Maalaa*
37.	Zircon	गोमेद	*Gomed*
38.	Vermilion	सिंदूर	*Sindoor*

World of Nature (प्रकृति का संसार)

	English	*हिंदी*	*Pronunciation*
1.	Air	हवा	*Hawaa*
2.	Continent	महाद्वीप	*Mahaadweepa*
3.	Cloud	बादल	*Baadal*
4.	Day	दिन	*Din*
5.	Evening	शाम	*Shaam*
6.	Earth	धरती	*Dhartee*
7.	Frost	पाला	*Paalaa*
8.	Fog	कोहरा	*Koharaa*
9.	Forest	जंगल	*Jungle*
10.	Fire	आग	*Aag*
11.	Gale	आँधी	*Aandhee*

12.	Heaven	स्वर्ग	*Swarg*
13.	Hell	नरक	*Narak*
14.	Hail	ओले	*Ole*
15.	Ice	बर्फ	*Barf*
16.	Land	ज़मीन/भूमि	*Zameen/Bhoomi*
17.	Lake	झील	*Jheel*
18.	Lightening	बिजली/विद्युत	*Bijalee/Vidyut*
19.	Moon	चांद	*Chaand*
20.	Milky way	आकाश गंगा	*Aakaash Gangaa*
21.	Mountain	पर्वत/पहाड़	*Parvata/Pahaad*
22.	Night	रात	*Raat*
23.	Ocean	महासागर	*Mahaasaagar*
24.	River	नदी	*Nadee*
25.	Sea	समुद्र/सागर	*Samudra/Saagar*
26.	Storm	तूफ़ान	*Toofaan*
27.	Shore	तट	*Tat*
28.	Shade	छाया	*Chhaayaa*
29.	Season	ऋतु	*Ritu*
30.	Stars	तारे	*Taare*
31.	Sky	आकाश/आसमान	*Aakaash Aasmaan*
32.	Tree	पेड़	*Pera*
33.	Water	पानी/जल	*Paanee/Jal*
34.	World	दुनिया	*Duniyaa/Sansaar*
35.	Water-fall	झरना	*Jharanaa*

❑❑❑

Chapter 10

Colours / Directions / Months / Planets/Seasons / Surroundings / Time denoting words / Weekdays

Name of Colours (रंगों के नाम)

	English	हिंदी	Pronunciation
1.	Brown	भूरा	*Bhooraa*
2.	Black	काला	*Kaalaa*
3.	Blue	नीला	*Neelaa*
4.	Bright	चमकीला	*Chamkeelaa*
5.	Blue-Black	स्याह नीला	*Syaah (Dark) Neelaa*
6.	Crimson	गहरा लाल	*Gehraa Laal*
7.	Gray	खाकी	*Khaakee*
8.	Green	हरा	*Haraa*
9.	Jet Black	स्याह काला	*Syaah(Dark) Kaalaa*
10.	Maroon	भूरा लाल	*Bhoora Laal*
11.	Orange	संतरी	*Santaree*
12.	Olive	मेहंदी	*Mehandee*
13.	Pink	गुलाबी	*Gulaabee*
14.	Purple	बैंगनी	*Benganee*
15.	Red	लाल	*Laal*
16.	Rosy	गुलाबी	*Gulaabee*

17. Scarlet	सिंदूरी	*Sindooree*
18. Violet	जामुनी	*Jaamunee*
19. White	सफेद	*Safed*
20. Yellow	पीला	*Peelaa*

Directions (दिशायें)

English	*हिंदी*	*Pronunciation*
1. East	पूर्व/पूरब	*Poorva/Poorab*
2. West	पश्चिम	*Pashchim*
3. North	उत्तर	*Uttar*
4. South	दक्षिण	*Dakshin*

Name of Months (महीनों के नाम)

English	*हिंदी*	*Pronunciation*
1. January	जनवरी	*Janavaree*
2. February	फरवरी	*Faravaree*
3. March	मार्च	*Maarch*
4. April	अप्रैल	*Aprail*
5. May	मई	*Mayee*
6. June	जून	*Joon*
7. July	जुलाई	*Julayee*
8. August	अगस्त	*Agasta*
9. September	सितम्बर	*Sitambar*
10. October	अक्टूबर	*Octoobar*
11. November	नवम्बर	*Navambar*
12. December	दिसम्बर	*Disambar*

Name of Planets (ग्रह)

	English	हिंदी	Pronunciation
1.	Earth	पृथ्वी	*Prithavee*
2.	Jupiter	बृहस्पति	*Brihaspati*
3.	Mars	मंगल	*Mangal*
4.	Mercury	बुध	*Budha*
5.	Naptune	वरूण	*Varuna*
6.	Pluto	प्लूटो	*Pluto*
7.	Saturn	शनि	*Shani*
8.	Uranus	यूरेनस	*Uranus*
9.	Venus	शुक्र	*Shukra*

Related to Season (मौसम संबंधी)

	English	हिंदी	Pronunciation
1.	Chill	ठंड	*Thand*
2.	Dust Storm	आंधी	*Aandhee*
3.	Hot	गर्म/गरम	*Garm/Garam*
4.	Humid	नम	*Nama*
5.	Rainy	बरसात	*Barsaat*
6.	Rain	बारिश	*Baarish*
7.	Storm	तूफान	*Toofaan*
8.	Spring	वसंत	*Vasant*
9.	Summer	गर्मी/गरमी	*Garmee*
10.	Sunshine	धूप	*Dhoop*
11.	Winter	सर्दी/सरदी	*Sardee*
12.	Wind	हवा	*Hawaa*

Surroundings (आसपास)

English	हिंदी	Pronunciation
1. Airport	हवाई अड्डा	*Hawaaee Addaa*
2. Aeroplane	हवाई जहाज़	*Hawaaee Jahaaz*
3. Bullock cart	बैलगाड़ी	*Bailgaaree*
4. Bar/Pub	बार/पब/	*Baar/ Pab/*
	शराबखाना	*Sharaabkhaanaa*
5. Country	देश	*Desha*
6 Church	गिरज़ाघर	*Girazaaghar*
7. Crowd	भीड़	*Bheera*
8. Crossing	चौराहा	*Chauraahaa*
9. Ditch	खाई	*Khaayee*
10. Electricity	बिजली	*Bijalee*
11. Farm	खेत/फार्म	*Khet/farm*
12. Field	मैदान	*Maidaan*
13. Factory	कारखाना	*Kaarkhaanaa*
14. Garden	बाग़	*Baag*
15. Gutter	नाला	*Naalaa*
16. Hut	झोंपड़ी	*Jhonpadee*
17. Highway	राजमार्ग	*Raajmaarga*
18. Hospital	चिकित्सालय	*Aspataal/*
		Chikitsaalaya
19. Inn	सराय	*Saraaye*
20. Land	ज़मीन	*Zameen*
21. Lane	गली	*Galee*
22. Library	पुस्तकालय	*Pustakaalaya*
23. Mosque	मस्जिद	*Maszid*
24. Market	बाज़ार	*Baazaar*
25. Orphange	अनाथालय	*Anaathaalaya*

26.	Office	दफ्तर	*Daftar*
27.	Post Office	डाकघर	*Daakaghar*
28.	Pole	खम्बा/खंभा	*Khambaa/ Khambha*
29.	Plant	पौधा	*Paudhaa*
30.	Palace	महल	*Mahal*
31.	Restaurant	रेस्तरां/भोजनालय	*Restaurant/ Bhojanaalaya*
32.	Road	सड़क	*Sadaka*
33.	State	राज्य	*Raajya*
34.	School	पाठशाला/विद्यालय	*Paathashaalaa/ Vidyaalaya*
35.	Shop	दुकान	*Dukaan*
36.	Station	स्टेशन/स्थानक	*Station/Sthaanak*
37.	Train	रेलगाड़ी	*Relagaaree*
38.	Tree	पेड़	*Per*
39.	Temple	मंदिर	*Mandir*
40.	Zoo	चिड़ियाघर	*Chiriyaaghar*

Time Denoting words (समयसूचक शब्द)

	English	*हिंदी*	*Pronunciation*
1.	After noon	दोपहर के बाद	*Dopahar ke Baad*
2.	Century	शताब्दी	*Shatabdee*
3.	Dawn	भोर	*Bhor*
4.	Day	दिन	*Din*
5.	Evening/Dusk	शाम	*Shaam*
6.	Fortnight	पखवाड़ा/पक्ष	*Pakhawaaraa/ Paksha*
7.	Hour	घण्टा	*Ghantaa*

	English	हिंदी	Pronunciation
8.	Mid Night	आधी रात	Aadhee Raat
9.	Minute	मिनट	Minute
10.	Morning	सुबह	Subah
11.	Night	रात	Raat
12.	Noon	दोपहर	Dopahar
13.	Month	मास/माह/महीना	Maas/Maah/ Maheena
14.	Second	सैकिण्ड	Second
15.	Time	समय/वक्त	Samay/Waqt
16.	Today	आज	Aaj
17.	Tonight	आज की रात	Aaj kee rat
18.	Tomorrow	आने वाला कल	Aane waalaa kal
19.	Week	सप्ताह/हफ्ता	Saptaah/Haftaa
20.	Year	वर्ष/बरस/साल	Varsha/Baras/ Saal
21.	Yesterday	बीता कल	Beetaa Kal

Days of the Weak (सप्ताह के दिनों के नाम)

	English	हिंदी	Pronunciation
1.	Sunday	इतवार/रविवार	Itwaar
2.	Monday	सोमवार	Somwaar
3.	Tuesday	मंगलवार	Mangalwaar
4.	Wednesday	बुधवार	Budhwaar
5.	Thursday	बृहस्पतिवार/ वीरवार/गुरूवार	Brihaspatiwa Veerwaar/ Guruwaar
6.	Friday	शुक्रवार	Shukrawaar
7.	Saturday	शनिवार	Shaniwaar

Chapter 11

Building & its parts / Household Articles

Building & its parts (भवन व इसके भाग)

English	हिंदी	Pronunciation
1. Bedroom	शयनकक्ष	Shayan kaksha
2. Bathroom	स्नानगृह/गुसलखाना	Snaangriha/gusalkhanaa
3. Balcony	बाल्कनी	Baalkoni
4. Battlement	मुंडेर	Munder
5. Beam	कड़ी	Karee
6. Brick	ईंट	Eenta
7. Bungalow	बंगला	Bangalaa
8. Courtyard	आंगन	Aangan
9. Cottage	झोंपड़ी	Jhonpadee
10. Ceiling	छत	Chhata
11. Dais	मचान/मंच	Machaan/Manch
12. Dining Room	खाने का कमरा	Khaane kaa Kamraa
13. Door	दरवाज़ा	Darvaazaa
14. Doorframe	चौखट	Chaukhat
15. Doorstep	दहलीज़	Dehaleez
16. Drain	नाली	Naalee
17. Drawing Room	बैठक कक्ष	Baithak Kaksha
18. Foundation	नींव	Neenva
19. Fountain	फव्वारा/फौहारा	Favvaaraa/fauhaaraa
20. Floor	फर्श	Farsh

	English	हिंदी	Pronunciation
21.	Guest Room	मेहमान का कमरा	*Mehmaan kaa Kamraa*
22.	House	घर	*Ghar*
23.	Kitchen	रसोई	*Rasoyee*
24.	Peehole	झरोखा	*Jharokhaa*
25.	Peg	खूँटी	*Khoontee*
26.	Roof	छत/छप्पर	*Chhata/ Chhappara*
27.	Room	कमरा	*Kamaraa*
28.	Storey	मंज़िल	*Manzil*
29.	Stair	सीढ़ी	*Seerhee*
30.	Swimming Pool	तरण ताल	*Taran Taal*
31.	Study Room	अध्ययन कक्ष	*Adhdhayan Kaksha*
32.	Toilet	शौचालय/टॉयलेट	*Shauchaalaya/ toilet*
33.	Verandah	बरामदा	*Baraamadaa*
34.	Window	खिड़की	*Khirkee*

Household Articles (घरेलू चीज़ें)

	English	*हिंदी*	*Pronunciation*
1.	Almirah	अलमारी	*Almaaree*
2.	Ash	राख	*Raakh*
3.	Ash -Tray	राखदानी	*Raakhdaanee*
4.	Axe	कुल्हाड़ी	*Kulhaaree*
5.	Basket	टोकरी	*Tokaree*
6.	Bed	पलंग	*Palang*
7.	Bedcover	पलंगपोश	*Palangposh*
8.	Bed sheet	चद्दर	*Chaddara*
9.	Bench	बेंच	*Bench*

10.	Bolster	मसनद	*Masanada*
11.	Bottle	बोतल	*Botal*
12.	Box	डिब्बा	*Dibbaa*
13.	Brush	ब्रुश	*Burush*
14.	Bracket	ब्रैकेट	*Bracket*
15.	Bucket	बाल्टी	*Baaltee*
16.	Broom	झाड़ू	*Jhaaroo*
17.	Bowl	कटोरा	*Katoraa*
18.	Blanket	कम्बल	*Kambal*
19.	Balance	तराजू	*Taraajoo*
20.	Button	बटन	*Batan*
21.	Chair	कुर्सी	*Kursee*
22.	Candle	मोमबत्ती	*Mombattee*
23.	Canister	कनस्तर	*Kanastar*
24.	Comb	कंघा	*Kanghaa*
25.	Cot	चारपाई	*Chaarpaayee*
26.	Carpet	कालीन	*Kaaleen*
27.	Cup	प्याला	*Pyaalaa*
28.	Cupboard	अलमारी	*Almaaree*
29.	Curtain	परदा	*Pardaa*
30.	Cauldron	कड़ाहा	*Karaahaa*
31.	Casket	सिंगारदान	*Singaardaan*
32.	Censer	धूपदानी	*Dhoopadaanee*
33.	Churner	मथनी	*Mathanee*
34.	Chain	जंज़ीर	*Zanzeer*
35.	Chimney	चिमनी	*Chimanee*
36.	Chandlier	फानूस	*Faanoos*
37.	Dish	पकवान/थाली	*Pakvaan/Thaalee*
38.	Divan	दीवान	*Divaan*

40.	Desk	डेस्क	*Desk*
41.	Flour	आटा	*Aatta*
42.	Funnel	कीप	*Keep*
43.	Fork	काँटा	*Kaantaa*
44.	Flower-vase	फूलदान	*Phooldaan*
45.	Fuel	ईंधन	*Indhan*
46	Grate	जाली	*Jaalee*
47.	Hearth	अंगीठी	*Angeethee*
48.	Hubble-bubble	हुक्का	*Hukkaa*
49.	Iron	इस्त्री	*Istree*
50.	Jar	मर्तबान	*Martabaan*
51.	Jug	सुराही/जग	*Suraahee/Jug*
52.	Key	चाबी	*Chaabee*
53.	Kerosene oil	मिट्टी का तेल	*Mittee kaa tel*
54.	Lock	ताला	*Taalaa*
55.	Lamp	दीया	*Deeyaa*
56.	Lotah	लोटा	*Lotaa*
57.	Lid	ढक्कन	*Dhhakkan*
58.	Ladle	चमचा/करछी	*Chamcha/Karchhee*
59.	Mat	चटाई	*Chataayee*
60.	Match-box	दियासलाई	*Diyaasalaayee*
61.	Mirror	शीशा	*Sheeshaa*
62.	Mortar	ओखली	*Okhalee*
63.	Match-stick	माचिस की तीली	*Maachis kee teelee*
64.	Needle	सुई	*Suyeen*
65.	Oven	तंदूर	*Tandoor*
66.	Palanquin	पालकी	*Paalakee*

67.	Pastry-board	चकला	*Chaklaa*
68.	Pen	लेखनी╱कलम	*Lekhanee/Kalam*
69.	Pestle	लोढ़ा╱मूसल	*Lorhaa/Moosal*
70.	Phial	शीशी	*Sheeshee*
71.	Pillow	तकिया	*Takiyaa*
72.	Plate	थाली	*Thaalee*
73.	Pincers	चिमटी╱चिमटा	*Chimtee/Chimtaa*
74.	Pot	हंडिया	*Handiyaa*
75.	Probe	सलाई	*Salaayee*
76.	Pitcher	घड़ा	*Gharaa*
77.	Pillow-cover	तकिये का गिलाफ़	*Takiye kaa gilaaf*
78.	Quilt	रज़ाई	*Razaayee*
79.	Rope	रस्सी	*Rassee*
80.	Radio	रेडियो	*Radio*
81.	Safe	तिज़ोरी	*Tizoree*
82.	Sieve	छलनी	*Chhalanee*
83.	Soap	साबुन	*Saabun*
84.	Sack	बोरा	*Boraa*
85.	Spitton	पीकदान	*Peekdaan*
86.	Spoon	चमचा╱चम्मच	*Chamchaa/ Chammach*
87.	Sofa Set	सोफा सेट	*Sofaa set*
88.	Stick	छड़ी	*Chharee*
89.	Stool	तिपाई╱स्टूल	*Tipaayee/stool*
90.	Stove	चूल्हा	*Choolhaa*
91.	String	रस्सी	*Rassee*
92.	Saucer	तश्तरी	*Tashtaree*
93.	Switch	स्विच	*Switch*

94.	Toothpick	दंत कुरेदनी	*Dant kuredanee*
95.	Tooth-powder	दंत मंजन	*Dant Manjan*
96.	Table	मेज़	*Mez*
97.	Thread	धागा	*Dhaagaa*
98.	Tap	नल	*Nal*
99.	Tumbler	गिलास	*Gilaas*
100.	Tonga	चिमटा	*Chimtaa*
101.	Tray	ट्रे	*Tray*
102.	Umbrella	छाता	*Chhaataa*
103.	Utensils	बर्तन	*Bartan*
104.	Wire	तार	*Taar*
105.	Wick	बत्ती	*Battee*

❑❑❑

Chapter 12

Army and War / Items of Stationary / Musical Instruments / Tools

Related to Army & War (सेना व लड़ाई संबंधी)

	English	हिंदी	Pronunciation
1.	Army	थल सेना	*Thal senaa*
2.	Airforce	वायु सेना	*Vaayu senaa*
3.	Attack	आक्रमण	*Aakramana*
4.	Atom bomb	अणु बम	*Anu bam*
5.	Bullet	गोली	*Golee*
6.	Battle	युद्ध	*Yuddha*
7.	Blockade	नाकाबन्दी	*Naakaabandee*
8.	Bloodshed	रक्तपात	*Raktapaat*
9.	Bomb	बम	*Bomb*
10.	Commander in chief	सेनापति	*Senaapati*
11.	Cease-Fire	युद्ध-विराम	*Yudha viraam*
12.	Cartridge	कारतूस	*Kaartoos*
13.	Civil-war	गृह युद्ध	*Griha yuddha*
14.	Cannon	तोप	*Top*
15.	Cold war	शीत युद्ध	*Sheet yuddha*
16.	Explosion	विस्फोटक	*Visphotak*
17.	Extrimist	आतंकवादी	*Aatankavaadee*
18.	Enemy	शत्रु/दुश्मन	*Shatru/Dushman*

	English	हिंदी	Pronunciation
19.	Gun	बंदूक	*Banddok*
20.	Navy	जल सेना	*Jal senaa*
21.	Prisoner of war	युद्धबन्दी	*Yudhabandee*
22.	Pistol	पिस्तौल	*Pistol*
23.	Submarine	पनडुब्बी	*Panadubbee*
24.	Treaty	सन्धि/सुलह	*Sandhi/sulaha*

Items of Stationery (लेखन-सामग्री)

	English	*हिंदी*	*Pronunciation*
1.	Book	किताब/पुस्तक	*Kitaab/Pustak*
2.	Blank paper	कोरा कागज	*Koraa Kaagaj*
3.	Blotting paper	स्याही चूस कागज	*Syaahee choos Kaagaj*
4.	Blue Ink	नीली स्याही	*Neelee syaahee*
5.	Black ink	काली स्याही	*Kaalee syaahee*
6.	Black board	ब्लैक बोर्ड	*Black Board*
7.	Bodkin	छेद करने का सुआँ	*Chhed karne kaa suan*
8.	Calling bell	घंटी	*Ghantee*
9.	Card	कार्ड	*Card*
10.	Clip	चिमटी	*Chimtee*
11.	Cork	कॉर्क	*Cork*
12.	Chalk	चॉक	*Chalk*
13.	Crayon	खड़िया पैंसिल	*Khariyaa Pencil*
14.	Carbon paper	कार्बन पेपर	*Carbon paper*
15.	Card board	गत्ता	*Gattaa*
16.	Divider	परकार	*Parkaar*
17.	Drawing pin	रेखण पिन	*Rekhan pin*

18.	Envelope	लिफाफा	*Lifaafaa*
19.	Eraser	रबड़	*Rabara*
20.	Exercise book	अभ्यास पुस्तिका	*Abhyaas Pustikaa*
21.	File	फाइल	*File*
22.	Gum	गोंद	*Gond*
23.	Glue	सरेस	*Sares*
24.	Holder	होल्डर	*Holder*
25.	Inkpot	दवात	*Dawaat*
26.	Ink	स्याही	*Syaahee*
27.	Invitation card	निमन्त्रण कार्ड	*Nimantran Card*
28.	Ink pad	स्याही पैड	*Syaahee ped*
29.	Knife	चाकू	*Chaakoo*
30.	Ledger	लेखा बही	*Lekhaa Bahee*
31.	Map	नक्शा	*Nakshaa*
33.	Nib	निब	*Nib*
34.	Paper	कागज़	*Kaagaz*
35.	Pen	पेन	*Pen*
36.	Pin	आलपिन	*Aalpin*
37.	Paper cutter	कागज़ तराश	*Kaagaz taraash*
38.	Paper weight	कागज दाब	*Kaagaz Daab*
39.	Pencil	पैंसिल	*Pencil*
40.	Packing paper	लपेटने का कागज़	*Lapetane kaa kaagaz*
41.	Pin cushion	आलपिन की गद्दी	*Aalpin kee gaddee*
42.	Punching Machine	छेद करने की मशीन	*Chhed karne kee machine*

43.	Quill pen	पर की कलम	*Par kee kalam*
44.	Register	पंजिका	*Panjikaa*
45.	Revenue stamp	रसीदी टिकट	*Raseedee ticket*
46.	Rubber band	रबड़ बैंड	*Rubber band*
47.	Rubber stamp	रबड़ की मोहर	*Rubber kee mohar*
48.	Receipt book	रसीद बही	*Raseed bahee*
49.	Ruler	फुट्टा/रेखक	*Phuttaa/Rekhak*
50.	Sharpener	पैंसिल छीलने वाला	*Pencil chheelane vaalaa*
51.	Slate	स्लेट	*Slate*
52.	Seal	मुहर	*Muhar*
53.	Sealing wax	लाख	*Laakh*
54.	Scissors	कैंची	*Kainchee*
55.	Stamp	मोहर/टिकट	*Mohar/Ticket*
56.	Stapler	स्टेपलर	*Stapler*
57.	Tag	डोरी	*Doree*
58.	Tape	फीता	*Feetaa*
59.	Tracing cloth	मोमी कपड़ा	*Momee kapadaa*
60.	Tracing paper	अक्स कागज	*Ax kaagaz*
61.	Visiting card	भेंट कार्ड	*Bhent card*
62.	Waste paper	रद्दी कागज	*Raddee kaagaz*
63.	Waste paper basket	रद्दी कागज की टोकरी	*Raddee kaagaz kee tokaree*
64.	Writing pad	लिखने का पैड	*Likhane kaa pad*
65.	Wire	तार	*Taar*

Musical Instruments (वाद्य यंत्र)

	English	हिंदी	Pronunciation
1.	Banjo	बैंजो	*Benjo*
2.	Bugle	बिगुल	*Bigul*
3.	Bongo	बोंगो	*Bongo*
4.	Bagpipe	बीन/मसकबाजा	*Been/Masakbaajaa*
5.	Congo	कोंगो	*Congo*
6.	Clarion	तुरही	*Turahee*
7.	Clarionet	शहनाई	*Shehanaayee*
8.	Cymbal	झांझ	*Jhanjh*
9.	Conch	शंख	*Shankh*
10.	Drum	ढोल	*Dhol*
11.	Drumet	डुगडुगी	*Dugdugee*
12.	Flute	बांसुरी	*Bansuree*
13.	Guitar	गिटार	*Gitaar*
14.	Harp	चंग	*Chang*
15.	Harmonium	हारमोनियम	*Haarmoniyam*
16.	Jews harp	मोरचंग	*Morchang*
17.	Piano	पियानो	*Piano*
18.	Sarod	सरोद	*Sarod*
19.	Sitar	सितार	*Sitaar*
20.	Sexaphone	सेक्साफोन	*Sexaphone*
21.	Synthesizer	सिंथेसाइजर	*Synthesizer*
22.	Tomtom	ढोलक	*Dholak*

English	हिंदी	Pronunciation
23. Tabor	तबला	*Tabalaa*
24. Tambourine	डफ/ढपली	*Daf/dhaplee*
25. Trumpt	ट्रम्पेट	*Trmpate*
26. Violin	वॉयलिन	*Violin*

Name of Tools (औजार)

English	हिंदी	Pronunciation
1. Axe	कुल्हाड़ी	*Kulhaaree*
2. Bead plane	गोल रंदा	*Gol randaa*
3. Balance	तराजू	*Taraazoo*
4. Bagging hook	दरांती	*Darantee*
5. Blade	ब्लेड	*Blade*
6. Cold chisel	छेनी	*Chhenee*
7. Cone	शंकु	*Shanku*
8. Compass	दिशासूचक	*Dishasoochak*
9. Drill Machine	छेदक मशीन	*Chhedak Machine*
10. File	रेती	*Reti*
11. Hammer	हथौड़ा	*Hathoraa*
12. Jackplane	रंदा	*Randaa*
13. Knife	चाकू/छुरी	*Chakoo/Churee*
14. Lever	उत्तोलक	*Uttolak*
15. Rudder	पतवार/चप्पू	*Patavaar/ Chappoo*
16. Plough	हल	*Hal*
17. Razor	उस्तरा	*Ustaraa*
18. Saw	आरी	*Aaree*

19.	Spade	कुदाल/फावड़ा	*Kudal/Faawadaa*
20.	Sickle	दरांती	*Darantee*
21.	Syringe	पिचकारी	*Pichkaaree*
22.	Screw	पेंच	*Pench*
23.	Spanner	पाना	*Panaa*
24.	Sickle	दरांती	*Darantee*
25.	Scissors	कैंची	*Kenchee*
26.	Screw driver	पेचकस	*Pechkas*

❏❏❏

Chapter 13

Common Sentences

So friends, by now you have learned the Hindi alphabets,their pronunciation, some basic rules relating to grammar and the common Hindi words in our daily use.

Hence, on the basis of this fundamental knowledge, now you may learn the formation of small sentences in Hindi as well as practice simple Hindi conversational exercises as per the tables given in this part.

Common Sentences for Everyday Use
(दैनिक उपयोग के सामान्य वाक्य)

1. Hello, how are you?
   हैलो, आप कैसे हैं?
   Hello, aap kaise hain?

2. I am fine
   मैं अच्छा हूँ
   Main achchhaa hoon.

3. Bring me coffee
   मेरे लिए कॉफी लाओ
   Mere liye coffee laao.

4. Please stay here
   यहाँ ठहरिये
   Yahaan theheriye.

5. Come here
   यहाँ आइये
   Yahaan aaiye.

6. Go inside
   अन्दर जाइये
   Andar jaaiye.

7. Please wait in the room
   कमरे में इन्तज़ार कीजिए
   Kamare mein intezaar keejiye.

8. Meet me at the office
   मुझसे दफ्तर में मिलिए
   Mujhse daftar mein miliye.

9. Take it
   यह लीजिए
   Yeha (ye) leejiye.

10. Give me paper
    मुझे कागज़ दीजिए
    Mujhe kaagaz deejiye.

11. I am outside
    मैं बाहर हूँ
    Main Baahar hoon.

12. Go upstairs
    ऊपर जाओ
    Oopar jaao.

13. Come down stairs
    नीचे आओ
    Neeche aao.

14. Call her quickly
उसे जल्दी बुलाओ
Use jaldi bulaao.

15. It is getting late
देर हो रही है
Der ho rahee hai.

16. Walk slowly
धीरे चलो
Dheere chalo.

17. Don't delay
देर मत कीजिए
Der mat keejiye.

18. I waited for you
मैंने तुम्हारा इंतज़ार किया
Maine tumhaaraa intezaar kiyaa.

19. Thank you
आपको धन्यवाद
Aapko dhanyavaad.

20. I need hair cut
मुझे बाल कटवाने हैं
Mujhe baal katvaane hain.

21. Why are you worried
तुम परेशान क्यों हो
Tum pareshaan kyon ho?

22. Which of these is yours
इनमें से कौन सा तुम्हारा है
Inmein se kaun sa tumhaaraa hai?

23. What is the matter
क्या बात है
Kyaa baat hai?

24. Where do you live
तुम कहाँ रहते हो
Tum kahaan rehte ho?

25. I am very glad to see you
आपको देखकर मुझे बहुत खुशी हुई
Aapko dekhkar mujhe bahut khushee huee.

26. The time is over
समय हो चुका है
Samay ho chukaa hai.

27. I am fond of singing
मुझे गाने का शौक है
Mujhe gaane kaa shauk hai.

28. I do not know him
मैं उसे नहीं जानता
Main use nahin jaantaa.

29. Where does Anil live
अनिल कहाँ रहता है?
Anil kahaan rehtaa hai?

30. What are you doing here
तुम यहाँ क्या कर रहे हो
Tum yahaan kyaa kar rahe ho.

31. Who has done it
यह किसने किया है
Yeh kisne kiyaa hai?

32. Do you understand
क्या तुम्हें समझ आया
Kyaa tumhen samajh aayaa?

33. Who has sent you
तुम्हें किसने भेजा है
Tumhen kisane bheja hai?

34. I am in a hurry
मैं ज़रा जल्दी मैं हूँ
Main zaraa jaldee main hoon.

35. What happeneed
क्या हुआ
Kyaa huaa?

36. I want to go to market
मुझे बाज़ार जाना है
Mujhe baazaar jaanaa hai

37. What is your name
तुम्हारा नाम क्या है
Tumhaaraa naam kyaa hai?

38. How old are you
तुम कितने साल के हो
Tum kitane saal ke ho?

39. Where do you live
तुम कहाँ रहते हो
Tum kahan rahate ho?

40. Who is your father
तुम्हारे पिता कौन हैं
Tumhaare pitaa kaun hain?

41. Which fruit do you like
तुम्हें कौन सा फल पसंद है
Tumhe kaun sa fal pasand hai?

42. What is your hobby
आपकी रुचि क्या है
Aapkee ruchi kyaa hai?

43. When do you get up
आप/तुम कब उठते हो
Aap/tum kab uthate ho?

44. Where is you office
आपका/तुम्हारा दफ्तर कहाँ है
Aapkaa/tumhaaraa daftar kahan hai?

45. How do you feel here
आपको यहाँ कैसा लगता है
Aapko yahaan kaisa lagtaa hai?

46. Why is the road closed
यह सड़क बंद क्यों है
Yeh sadak band kyon hai?

47. What do you mean
तुम्हारा/आपका क्या मतलब है
Tumhaaraa/aapkaa kyaa matlab hai?

48. What is the matter
क्या बात है
Kyaa baat hai?

49. He needs you
उसे तुम्हारी ज़रूरत है
Use tumhaaree zaroorat hai.

50. My name is John
मेरा नाम जॉन है
Meraa naam John hai?

51. Follow me
मेरे पीछे आओ
Mere peechhe aao.

52. This is my house
ये मेरा घर है
Ye meraa ghar hai.

53. Work is finished
काम पूरा हुआ
kaam poora hua.

54. When do we meet again?
हम फिर कब मिलेंगे
Ham phir kab milenge?

55. Are you a student?
क्या तुम पढ़ते/पढ़ती हो
Kya tum padhte/padhtee ho?

56. I have to go
मुझे जाना है
Mujhe jaanaa hai.

57. I am getting late
मुझे देर हो रही है
Mujhe dair ho rahee hai.

ロロロ

Chapter 14

Greetings / Invitation / Meeting and Parting / Gratitude / Congratulations and Good Wishes / Request / Permission / Instructions

Common Greetings (सामान्य अभिवादन)

English	हिंदी	Pronunciation
1. Good morning	सुप्रभात	*Suprabhaat*
2. Good noon	शुभ दोपहर	*Shubh dopahar*
3. Good day	शुभ दिवस/दिन	*Shubh divas/din*
4. Good evening	शुभ संध्या	*Shubh sandhyaa*
5. Good night	शुभ रात्रि	*Shubh ratree*
6. Namaste	नमस्ते	*Namaste*
7. Namaskar	नमस्कार	*Namaskaar*
8. O.K.	ठीक है/ओके	*Theek hai/ok*
9. Bye	विदा	*Vidaa*
10. Thank you	धन्यवाद	*Dhanyavaad*
11. Welcome	स्वागत	*Swaagat*
12. Hello	हैलो	*Hello*
13. Hi	हाय	*Hi*
14. See you	फिर मिलेंगे	*Phir Milenge*

Invitation / आमंत्रण

1. Come in please
   कृपया अन्दर आइये
   Kripayaa andar aaiye.

2. Please have a cold drink
   कृपया कुछ ठण्डा लीजिए
   Kripayaa kuchchha thandaa leejiye.

3. Come for a walk please
   कृपया टहलने के लिए आइये
   Kripayaa tehalne ke liye aaiye.

4. Would you like to see movie
   क्या तुम मूवी देखना चाहोगे
   Kyaa tum movie dekhanaa chaahoge?

5. Let us go by taxi
   आओ टैक्सी से चलें
   Aao taxi se chalen.

6. Here is an invitation card for you
   आपके लिए निमंत्रण पत्र आया है
   Aapke liye nimantrana patra aayaa hai.

7. Thanks for your invitation
   आपके निमंत्रण के लिए धन्यवाद
   Aapke nimantran ke liye dhanyavaad.

Meeting and Parting / भेंट और विदा

1. Hello friend! how are you
   कहो दोस्त कैसे हो
   Kaho dost kaise ho?

2. I am fine by God's grace
   भगवान की कृपा से मैं ठीक हूँ
   Bhagwaan kee kripaa se main theek hoon.

3. I am very happy to see you
   आपसे मिलकर मुझे बहुत खुशी हुई
   Aapse milkar mujhe bahut khushee huee.

4. This is my pleaseure
   यह मेरे लिए खुशी की बात है
   Yeha mere liye khushee kee baat hai.

5. Have a happy journey
   आपकी यात्रा अच्छी हो
   Aapkee yatraa achchhee ho!

6. God bless you
   ईश्वर आप पर कृपा करे
   Ishwar aap par kripaa kare!

7. May luck favour you
   भाग्य आपका साथ दे
   Bhaagya aapkaa saath de!

8. What can I do for you
   मैं आपके लिए क्या कर सकता हूँ
   Main aapke liye kyaa kar saktaa hoon?

9. O key, we will meet again
   अच्छा हम फिर मिलेंगे
   Achchhaa, hum phir milenge.

10. Thank you for your help
    आपकी मदद के लिए धन्यवाद
    Aapkee madad ke liye dhanyavaad!

Gratitude / आभार

1. Many thanks
   बहुत धन्यवाद
   Bahut dhanyavaad

2. Thanks for your advice
   आपकी सलाह के लिए धन्यवाद
   Aapkee salaaha ke liye dhanyavaad.

3. Thanks for this present
   इस उपहार के लिए धन्यवाद
   Is uphaar ke liye dhanyavaad.

4. I am very grateful to you
   मैं आपका बहुत आभारी हूँ
   Main aapkaa bahut aabhaaree hoon.

5. You are very kind
   आप बहुत दयालु हैं
   Aap bahut dayaaloo hain.

Congratulations & Good Wishes / बधाई एवं शुभकामनाएं

1. Wish you a happy new year
   आपको नए साल की शुभकामनाएँ
   Aapko naye saal ke shubh kaamanaayein.

2. Heartist congratulations on your birthday
   आपको जन्मदिन पर हार्दिक बधाई
   Aapko janmadin per haardik badhaaee.

3. Many happy returns of the day
   यह दिन बार-बार आए
   Yeha din baar-baar aaye.

1. Congratulations on your success
आपकी सफलता पर बधाई
Aapkee saflataa par badhaaee.

5. Congratulations on your wedding
आपके विवाह पर बधाई
Aapke vivaaha par badhaaee.

6. I wish your success in your work
मैं आपके काम की सफलता की कामना करता हूँ
Main aapke kaam kee safalataa kee kaamanaa karataa hoon.

Request / प्रार्थना

1. Please wait
ज़रा ठहरिये
Zaraa thehariye.

2. Please come back
वापस आइये
Vaapas aaiye.

3. Please reply
उत्तर दीजिए
Uttar deejiye.

4. Will you do me a favour
मेरा एक काम करोगे
Meraa ek kaam karoge?

5. Let me work
मुझे काम करने दो
Mujhe kaam karne do.

6. Let me see
   ज़रा देखने दो/मैं देखता हूँ
   Zaraa dekhane do/main dekhataa hoon.

7. Please repeat
   कृपया फिर से कहिए/दोबारा कहिए
   Kripaya phir se kahiye / Dobaaraa kahiye.

8. Let him relex
   उसे आराम करने दीजिए
   Use aaraam karne deejiye.

Permission / आज्ञा

1. May I go
   मैं जा सकता हूँ
   Main jaa sakataa hoon?

2. You may go
   तुम जा सकते हो
   Tum jaa sakate ho.

3. May I join you
   मैं शामिल हो सकता हूँ
   Main shaamil ho sakataa hoon?

4. May I use your telephone
   क्या मैं आपका टेलीफोन इस्तेमाल कर सकता हूँ
   Kyaa main aapkaa telephone istemaal kar sakataa hoon?

5. May I come in
   क्या मैं अन्दर आ सकता हूँ
   Kyaa main andar aa sakataa hoon?

Instructions / निर्देश

1. Go yourself
   तुम ही जाओ
   Tum hee jaao.

2. Be ready
   तैयार रहो
   Taiyaar raho.

3. Switch on the light
   बिजली जला दो
   Bijalee jalaa do.

4. Switch off the light
   बिजली बुझा दो
   Bijalee bujhaa do.

5. Wash your hands
   अपने हाथ धो लो
   Apne haath dho lo.

6. Come soon
   जल्दी आना
   Jaldee aanaa.

7. Go back
   वापिस जाओ
   Vaapis jaao.

8. Don't delay
   देर मत करो
   Der mat karo.

9. Do not do so in future
   आगे से ऐसा मत करना
   Aage se aisaa mat karnaa.

10. Post this letter
    यह पत्र डाल दो
    Yeha patra daal do.

11. Be punctual
    समय का पालन करो
    Samaya kaa paalan karo.

12. Give up bad habits
    खराब आदतें छोड़ दो
    Kharaab aadatain chhod do.

13. Don't chatter
    बक-बक ना करो
    Bak-bak naa karo.

14. Mind your business
    अपना काम करो
    Apnaa kaam karo.

15. Talk politely
    नरमी से बात करो
    Naramee se baat karo.

16. Respect your elders
    बड़ों का आदर करो
    Badon kaa aadar karo.

17. Be aware of pick-pockets
    ज़ेबकतरों से बचो
    Zebkatron se bacho.

18. Take off your shoes
अपने जूते उतार दो
Apne joote utaar do.

19. Unpack the luggage
सामान खोल दो
Saamaan khol do.

20. Make the bed
बिस्तर लगा दो
Bistar lagaa do.

21. Peel off the oranges
संतरों को छील दो
Santaron ko cheel do.

22. Sink your differences
अपना झगड़ा निपटा दो
Apnaa jhagraa niptaa do.

23. Sit on the chair
कुर्सी पर बैठो
Kursee par baitho.

24. Now keep quiet
अब चुप हो जाओ
Ab chup ho jao.

25. Have you meals
अपना खाना खा लो
Apnaa Khaana khaa lo.

❑❑❑

Chapter 15

Encouragement and Consent /Anger and Quarrel /Apologies / Time / Weather /Education / Health / So me Do's / Some Don'ts

Encourgement & Consent / प्रोत्साहन व सहमति

1. Rest assured
   विश्वास रखिए
   Vishwaas rakhiye.

2. Don't worry
   चिन्ता मत करो
   Chintaa mat karo.

3. Don't hesitate
   संकोच मत करो
   Sankoch mat karo.

4. Don't get nervous
   घबराओ मत
   Ghabaraao mat.

5. Bravo! well done
   शाबाश, बहुत अच्छा!
   Shaabaash, bahut achchhaa!

6. That's wonderful
कमाल कर दिया
Kamaal kar diyaa.

7. As you like
जैसी तुम्हारी मर्ज़ी
Jaisee tumharee marzee.

8. This is quite right
यह बिल्कुल ठीक है
Yeh bilkul theek hai.

9. I agree
मैं सहमत हूँ
Main sehamat hoon.

10. It does not matter
कोई हर्ज़ नहीं
Koee harz nahin.

Anger & Quarrel / गुस्सा व झगड़ा

1. Why are you losing temper
आप गुस्सा क्यों हो रहे हो
Aap gussaa kyon ho rahe ho?

2. You are very short tempered
तुम्हारा गुस्सा बहुत तेज़ है
Tumhaaraa gussaa bahut tez hai.

3. Do not be excited
गुस्सा मत करो
Gussaa mat karo.

4. Go to hell
   भाड़ में जाओ
   Bhaad mein jaao.

5. Are you in your senses
   क्या आप होश में हैं
   Kyaa aap hosh mein hain.

6. Shame on you
   लानत है तुम पर
   Laanat hai tum par!

7. You are a slippery character
   तुम बड़े चालू आदमी हो
   Tum bade chaaloo aadmee ho.

Apologies / क्षमायाचना

1. Are you angry
   क्या आप नाराज हो
   Kyaa aap naaraaj ho?

2. I was just joking
   मैं तो मज़ाक कर रहा था
   Main to mazaak kar rahaa thaa.

3. I beg your pardon
   मैं तुमसे माफी चाहता हूँ
   Mein tumse maafee chaahataa hoon.

4. I am very sorry
   मुझे बहुत अफ़सोस है
   Mujhe bahut afsos hai.

5. Make my apologies
   मेरी ओर से माफी माँग लीजिए
   Meree ore se mafee maang leejiye.

Time / समय

1. What is the time
   क्या बजा है/कितने बजे हैं
   Kyaa bajaa hai/kitane baje hain?

2. It is half past seven
   साढ़े सात बजे हैं
   Saadhe saat baje hain.

3. When do you go to school
   तुम स्कूल कब जाते हो
   Tum school kab jaate ho?

4. I go to school at nine'o clock
   मैं नौ बजे स्कूल जाता हूँ
   Mein nau baje school jaataa hoon.

5. When do you have your morning tea
   तुम सुबह की चाय कब पीते हो
   Tum subah kee chaya kab peete ho?

6. I have my tea at quarter past seven
   मैं सवा सात बजे चाय पीता हूँ
   Mein savaa saat baje chaya peetaa hoon.

7. I start study at quarter to four
   मैं पौने चार बजे पढ़ना शुरू करता हूँ
   Mein paune chaar baje padhnaa shuroo kartaa hoon.

8. It's ten past three now
   इस वक्त तीन बजकर दस मिनट हुए हैं
   Is waqt teen bajkar dus minute huye hain.

9. I have to go at twenty to four
   मुझे चार बजने से बीस मिनट पहले जाना है
   Mujhe chaar bajne se bees minute pehle jaana hai.

10. What is the date today
    आज क्या तारीख है
    Aaj kyaa taareekh hai?

11. It is time to get up
    उठने का समय हो गया है
    Uthane ka samaya ho gayaa hai.

12. We have enough time
    हमारे पास बहुत समय है
    Hamaare paas bahut samaya hai.

13. It is nearly mid night
    क़रीब आधी रात है
    Qareeb aadhee raat hai.

14. Better times will come
    अच्छे दिन आएँगे
    Achchhe din aayenge.

15. Your watch is ten minutes fast
    तुम्हारी घड़ी दस मिनट आगे है
    Tumhaaree ghadee dus minute aage hai.

16. My watch is five minutes slow
    मेरी घड़ी पाँच मिनट पीछे है
    Meri ghadee paanch minute peechhe hai.

Weather / मौसम

1. It is very pleasent today
   आज मौसम बहुत सुहाना है
   Aaj mausam bahut suhaanaa hai.

2. It is close today
   आज हवा बंद है
   Aaj hawaa band hai.

3. It is hot today
   आज गर्मी है
   Aaj garmee hai.

4. Summer is in full swing
   गर्मी पूरे जोरों पर है
   Garmee poore joron par hai.

5. The clouds are thundering
   बादल गरज रहे हैं
   Baadal garaj rahe hain.

6. The lightning is flashing
   बिजली चमक रही है
   Bijalee chamak rahee hai.

7. The sky is overcast with clouds
   आकाश में बादल छाये हैं
   Aakaash mein baadal chhaaye hain.

8. It is drizzling
   बूँदा-बाँदी हो रही है
   Boondaa baandee ho rahee hai.

9. It is raining cats and dogs
मूसलाधार बारिश हो रही है
Mooslaadhaar baarish ho rahi hai.

Education / शिक्षा

1. Illiteracy is a curse
निरक्षरता अभिशाप है
Nirakshartaa abhishaap hai.

2. A man without educatiuon is not less than an animal
विद्या के बिना मनुष्य पशु के समान है
Vidyaa ke binaa manushya pashu ke samaan hai.

3. The school shall remain closed tomorrow
कल विद्यालय बंद रहेगा
Kal vidyaalya band rahegaa.

4. The teacher called the roll
अध्यापक ने हाज़िरी ली
Addhyaapak ne haaziree lee.

5. He falls short of attendance
उसकी हाज़रियां कम हैं
Uskee haazriyaan kam hain.

Health / स्वास्थ्य (सेहत)

1. How do you do
आप कैसे हैं
Aap kaise hain?

2. I feel no appetite
मुझे भूख नहीं लगती
Mujhe bhookh nahin lagtee.

3. He is feeling giddy
उसका सिर चकरा रहा है
Uskaa sir chakaraa rahaa hai.

4. He is blind
वह अंधा है
Wah andhaa hai.

5. He is hard of hearing
उसे ऊँचा सुनाई देता है
Use oonchaa sunaaee detaa hai.

Some do's / कुछ करने योग्य बातें

1. Do a noble act everyday
रोज एक अच्छा काम करो
Roj ek achchhaa kaam karo.

2. Brush your teeth daily
अपने दाँत रोज साफ करो
Apne daant roj saaf karo.

3. Go out for a walk daily
रोज सैर को जाओ
Roj sair ko jaao.

4. Help the poor
गरीबों की सहायता करो
Gareebon kee sahaayataa karo.

5. Work hard
मेहनत करो
Mehnat karo.

6. Be honest
   ईमानदार बनो
   Imaandaar bano.

7. Be punctual
   समय के पाबंद रहो
   Samaya ke paaband raho.

8. Speak always truth
   सदा सच बोलो
   Sadaa such bolo.

9. Trust in god
   ईश्वर पर भरोसा रखो
   Ishwar par bharosaa rakho.

10. Be true to your word
    अपने वचनों का पालन करो
    Apne vachanon kaa paalan karo.

11. Obey your parents
    माता-पिता की आज्ञा मानो
    Maataa-pitaa kee aagyaa maano.

12. Remain neat and clean
    साफ-सुथरे रहो
    Saaf-suthare raho.

13. Do exercise daily
    रोजाना कसरत करो
    Rojaanaa kasrat karo.

14. Follow the rules
    नियमों का पालन करो
    Niyamon kaa paalan karo.

15. Get up early in the morning
सुबह जल्दी उठो
Subaha jaldi utho.

Some don'ts / कुछ ना करने वाली बातें

1. Don't waste your time
अपना समय नष्ट मत करो
Apnaa samaya nasht mat karo.

2. Don't smoke
धूम्रपान मत करो
Dhumrapaan mat karo.

3. Don't tease any body
किसी को मत चिढ़ाओ
Kisee ko mat chidhaao.

4. Don't tell a lie
झूठ मत बोलो
Jhooth mat bolo.

5. Don't gamble
जुआ मत खेलो
Juaa mat khelo.

6. Don't back-bite others
दूसरों की चुगली मत करो
Doosron kee chugalee mat karo.

7. Don't sit idle
खाली मत बैठो
Khaalee mat baitho.

8. Don't torment anybody
   किसी को मत सताओ
   Kisee ko mat sataao.

9. Don't spit on the floor
   फर्श पर मत थूको
   Farsh par mat thooko.

10. Don't abuse anybody
    किसी को गाली मत दो
    Kisee ko gaalee mat do.

11. Don't get up late
    देरी से मत उठो
    Deree se mat utho.

12. Don't sleep in the day
    दिन में मत सो
    Din mein mat so.

13. Don't bite your nails
    अपने नाखून दाँतों से मत काटो
    Apne naakhoon daanton se mat kaato.

14. Don't cheat any body
    किसी को धोखा मत दो
    Kisee ko dhokhaa mat do.

15. Don't make fun of anybody
    किसी का मज़ाक मत बनाओ
    Kisee kaa mazaak mat banaao.

❏❏❏

Chapter 16

Important Conversations—On arrival / Tourist office / Railway Station / Enquiry at Station / At Bus Stop/ As Guest / At the Shop / With Taxi Driver /At a Hotel

On Arrival / पहुँचने पर

John— Hello, Gentleman, can you help me?
हैलो जनाब, क्या आप मेरी मदद कर सकते हैं?
Hello janaab, kyaa aap meree madad kar sakate hain?

P.K.— Yes, why not?
हाँ, क्यों नहीं?
Haan, kyon naheen?

John— I am John from Australia and I am a tourist.
मैं आस्ट्रेलिया से जॉन हूँ और मैं एक पर्यटक हूँ।
Main Australia se John hoon aur main ek paryatak hoon.

P.K.— Oh! welcome to India. I am P.K.
ओह! भारत में आपका स्वागत है, मैं पी.के. हूँ।
Oh! Bhaarat mein aapkaa swaagat hai, main P.K. hoon.

John— Please tell me where could I stay in Delhi?
कृपया मुझे बताइये कि दिल्ली में मैं कहाँ ठहर सकता हूँ?
Kripaya mujhe bataaiye ki Delhi mein, main kahaan thehar sakataa hoon?

P.K.— There are many good hotels.
यहाँ कई अच्छे होटल हैं।
Yahaan kaee achchhe hotel hain.

John— Please tell me any nearby good hotel.
कृपया मुझे पास में कोई अच्छा होटल बताइये।
Kripayaa mujhe pass mein koee achchha hotel bataaiye.

P.K.— You may stay at Taj Hotel.
आप ताज होटल में ठहर सकते हैं।
Aap Taj Hotel mein thehar Sakte hain.

John— O.K.! Thanks a lot for this information.
ठीक है! ये जानकारी देने के लिए आपका बहुत धन्यवाद।
Theek hai! ye jaankaaree dene ke liye aapakaa bahut dhanyavaad.

P.K.— Bye! Have a nice time in India.
अलविदा! भारत में आपका समय अच्छा बीते।
Alavidaa! Bhaarat mein aapakaa samaya achchhaa beete.

In the Tourist Office / यात्री कार्यालय में

John— What places of tourist interest are in Delhi?
दिल्ली में कौन-कौन से स्थान देखने लायक हैं?
Delhi mein kaun-kaun se sthaan dekhne laayak hain?

PRO— There are many places to visit, what would you like to see?

यहाँ देखने लायक बहुत से स्थान हैं, आप क्या देखना चाहेंगे?

Yahaan dekhne laayak bahut ses sthaan hain, aap kyaa dekhnaa chaahenge?

John— I would like to see Lal Quila.

मैं लाल किला देखना चाहता हूँ।

Main Lal Quilaa dekhnaa chaahtaa hoon.

What is the best conveyance to go there?

वहाँ पहुँचने का सबसे अच्छा साधन क्या है?

Wahaan pahunchne kaa sabse achchhaa saadhan kyaa hai?

PRO— You can go by auto or taxi.

आप ऑटो या टैक्सी से जा सकते हैं।

Aap auto yaa taxi se jaa sakte hain.

John— Can I get there a guide?

क्या वहाँ मुझे गाइड मिल पाएगा?

Kyaa wahaan mujhe guide mil paayegaa?

PRO— Of course.

बिल्कुल जनाब।

Bilkul janaab.

Jonh— Can I take photographs there?

क्या मैं वहाँ फोटो खींच सकता हूँ?

Kyaa main wahaan photo kheench sakataa hoon?

PRO— Yes please.

जी हाँ।

Jee haan.

John— O.K. I am going there, thank you.
ठीक है, मैं वहाँ जा रहा हूँ, धन्यवाद।
Theek hai, main wahaan jaa rahaa hoon,
dhanyavaad.

At a Railway Station / रेलवे स्टेशन पर

John— May I know your name?
तुम्हारा नाम क्या है?
Tumhaaraa naam kyaa kai?

Rosy— My name is Rosy.
मेरा नाम रोज़ी है।
Meraa naam Rosy hai.

John— Where are you going?
आप कहाँ जा रही हैं?
Aap kahaan jaa rahee hain?

Rosy— I am going to Mumbai.
मैं मुंबई जा रही हूँ।
Main Mumbai jaa rahee hoon.

John— How long will the train take to reach there?
गाड़ी को वहाँ पहुँचने में कितना समय लगेगा?
Gaadee ko wahaan pahunchne mein kitnaa
samay lagegaa?

Rosy— About 18 hours.
लगभग 18 घंटे।
Lagbhag 18 ghante. •

John— Where will you stay there?
आप वहाँ कहाँ रहेंगी?
Aap wahaan kahaan rahengee?

Rosy—   In a Hotel.

होटल में।

IIotel mein.

John—   Could you suggest me some places which I may visit?

क्या घूमने के लिए आप कुछ स्थान बताने की कृपा करेंगी?

Kyaa ghoomne ke liye aap kuchha sthaan bataane kee kripaa karengee?

Rosy—   Why not ! If you like, I shall be too glad to accompany you.

क्यों नहीं ! आप चाहेंगे तो आपका साथ देने में मुझे खुशी होगी।

Kyon naheen ! Aap chaahenge to aapkaa saath dene mein mujhe khushee hogee.

John—   Thanks a lot!

बहुत-बहुत धन्यवाद!

Bahut-bahut dhanyavaad!

Enquiry at Station / स्टेशन पर पूछताछ

John—   When does the Mumbai-bound train arrived?

मुंबई जाने वाली गाड़ी कब आती है?

Mumbai jaane waalee gaadee kab aatee hai?

Clerk—   At quarter past four sir.

सवा चार बजे महोदय।

Savaa chaar baje mahodaya.

John—   On which platform and its departure time?

किस प्लेटफॉर्म पर और कितने बजे?

Kis platform par aur kitne baje?

Clerk— On platform No. 3 and it leaves at quarter to five.

प्लेटफॉर्म नं. 3 से पौने पाँच बजे जाती है।

Platform No.3 se paune paanch baje jaatee hai.

John— Coolie, please carry my luggage to platform No. 3.

कुली, मेरा सामान प्लेटफॉर्म नं. 3 तक ले चलो।

Coolie, meraa saamaan platform No.3 tak le chalo.

John— Would you please move a little?

क्या आप कुछ खिसकेंगे?

Kyaa aap kuchha khiskenge?

Pass. II— Of course, why not?

बिल्कुल, क्यों नहीं?

Bilkul, kyon naheen?

Porter— Sir, please pay Rs. 20 as my charges.

साहब, मेरे भाड़े के 20 रुपये दीजिए।

Saahab, mere bhaade ke 20 rupaye dijiye.

John— This is too much, take Rs. 15.

ये तो बहुत ज्यादा है, 15 रुपये ले लो।

Ye to bahut jyaadaa hai, 15 rupaye le lo.

Porter— No sir, your luggage is heavy. Please give Rs. 20 sir, I am a poor man.

नहीं साहब, आपका सामान बहुत भारी है। साहब कृपा करके 20 रुपये दे दीजिए, मैं गरीब आदमी हूँ।

Naheen saahab , aapke suamaan bahut bhaari hai. Saahab kripa karke 20 rupaye de deejiye, main gareeb aadmee hoon.

John—	O.K., keep this Rs. twenty.
	ठीक है, ये बीस रुपये रखो।
	Theek hai, ye bees rupaye rakho.

At Bus Stop / बस स्टॉप पर

John—	Will you please tell me the bus stop for Connaught Place?
	क्या आप मुझे कनॉट प्लेस जाने के लिए बस स्टॉप बता सकेंगे?
	Kyaa aap mujhe Connaught Place jaane ke liye bus stop bataa sakenga?
By stander—	This is the right Bus Stop.
	यह सही बस स्टॉप है।
	Yaha sahee Bus Stop hai.
John—	How long does it take to reach Connaught Place?
	कनॉट प्लेस पहुँचने में कितना समय लगता है?
	Connaught Place pahunchne mein kitnaa samay lagtaa hai?
By stander—	Hardly, 20 minutes sir.
	मुश्किल से 20 मिनट महोदय।
	Mushkila se 20 minute mahadaya.
John—	When will the next bus come?
	अगली बस कब आयेगी?
	Aglee bus kab aayegee?

By stander— It is difficult to say. It may come in ten to fifteen minutes.

यह कहना तो मुश्किल है। दस से पंद्रह मिनट में आ सकती है।

Yaha kehnaa to mushkil hai. Dus se pandraha minute mein aa saktee hai.

John— But I have the impression that buses are not so punctual.

लेकिन मेरा ख्याल तो ये है कि बसें नियमित नहीं हैं।

Lekin meraa khyaal to ye hai ki basein niyamit naheen hain.

By stander— No, now this is not so.

नहीं, अब ऐसा नहीं है।

Naheen, ab aisaa naheen hai.

John— Let us see.

चलिए, देखते हैं।

Chaliye, dekhte hain.

By stander— Look, there is your bus ! Get into it quickly.

वह देखिये, आपकी बस ! जल्दी से चढ़ जाइये।

Waha dekhiye, aapkee bus ! Jaldee se chadh jaaiye.

John— Thank you ! Bye-bye.

धन्यवाद! नमस्ते।

Dhanyavaad ! Namaste.

As Guest / बतौर मेहमान

Ram — Here you all ! Why all alone? Where is your wife?
आप आ गए! अकेले क्यों? आपकी पत्नी कहाँ है?
Aap aa gaye ! Akele kyon? Aapkee patnee kahaan hai?

John — At the very moment of departure, she changed her mind. Next time she will certainly come.
चलते समय उसका इरादा बदल गया। अगली बार वह जरूर आयेगी।
Chalte samay uskaa iraadaa badal gayaa. Aglee baar waha jaroor aayegee.

Ram — Well, have a seat ! Would you take tea or coffee?
अच्छा, बैठिये! चाय लेंगे या कॉफी?
Achchhaa, baithiye ! chaaye leinge yaa coffee?

John — Coffee will do.
कॉफी चलेगी।
Coffee chalegee.

Ram — How was the journey? Was the bus crowded?
आपकी यात्रा कैसी रही? क्या बस में भीड़ थी?
Aapkee yaatra kaisee rahee? Kyaa bus mein bheed thee?

John — Yes it was, but I got the seat.
हाँ थी, लेकिन मुझे सीट मिल गई थी।
Haan thee, lekin mujhe seat mil gaee thee.

Ram—   That's good.
ये अच्छा हुआ।
Ye achchhaa huaa.

John—   Well, I think I should have a bath right now.
अच्छा, मेरे ख्याल से अब मुझे नहा लेना चाहिए।
Achchhaa, mere khyaal se ab mujhe nahaa lenaa chaahiye.

Ram—   Of course, take a hot bath.
बिल्कुल, गरम पानी से नहा लें।
Bilkul, garam paanee se nahaa lein.

John—   I am dead tired and I want to sleep.
मैं बुरी तरह से थका हुआ हूँ और अब सोना चाहता हूँ।
Main buree taraha se thakaa huaa hoon aur ab sonaa chaahtaa hoon.

Ram—   Of course not, you have to take dinner first. It will refresh you.
अरे, बिल्कुल नहीं, आपको पहले रात का भोजन लेना है। इससे आपकी थकान दूर हो जायेगी।
Arei, bilkul naheen, aapko pahale raat kaa bhojan lenaa hai. Isse aapkee thakaan door ho jaayegee.

At the Shop / दुकान पर

Shopkeeper—   Yes sir, what would you like to have?
श्रीमान आप क्या लेना चाहेंगे?
Shreemaan aap kyaa lenaa chaahenge?

John—	I have come to buy a book.
	मैं एक किताब लेने आया हूँ।
	Main ek kitaab lene aayaa hoon.
Shopkeeper—	Let me know the title please?
	कृपया नाम बताइये?
	Kripayaa naam bataiye?
John—	I want to learn Hindi.
	मैं हिन्दी सीखना चाहता हूँ।
	Main Hindi seekhnaa chaahtaa hoon.
Shopkeeper—	Yes, I have a popular book for learning and speaking Hindi.
	हाँ, मेरे पास हिंदी सीखने और बोलने के लिए एक प्रसिद्ध पुस्तक है।
	Haan, mere paas Hindi seekhne aur bolne ke liye ek prasiddha pustak hai.
John—	Is it really so good?
	क्या यह वाकई बहुत अच्छी है?
	Kyaa yeh vaquee bahut achchhe hai?
Shopkeeper—	Yes of course, it is selling like hot cake.
	हाँ, यह तो हाथोंहाथ बिक रही है।
	Haan, yeh to haathonhaath bik rahi hai.
John—	O.K. Give me this book.
	ठीक है, मुझे यह पुस्तक दे दीजिए।
	Theek hai, mujhe yeh pustak de deejiye.
Shopkeeper—	Thank you!
	धन्यवाद!
	Dhanyavaad!

With Taxi driver / टैक्सी चालक से

John—
Taxi!
टैक्सी!
Taxi!

Taxi Driver—
Yes, sir.
हाँ, साहब।
Haan, saahab.

John—
Drive me to Taj Hotel.
मुझे ताज होटल ले चलो।
Mujhe Taj Hotel le chalo.

Taxi Driver—
Get in sir.
चलिए साहब।
Chaliye saahab.

John—
How far is Taj Hotel from here?
यहाँ से ताज होटल कितनी दूर है?
Yahaan se Taj Hotel kitanee door hai?

Taxi Driver—
About ten k.m. sir.
करीब दस किलोमीटर जनाब।
Kareeb das k.m. janaab.

John—
How much charges I have to pay?
मुझे कितना किराया देना होगा?
Mujhe kitnaa kiraayaa denaa hoga?

Taxi Driver—
I will charge according to this rate list.
मैं इस रेट लिस्ट के हिसाब से किराया लूँगा।
*Main is rate list ke hisaab se
kiraaya loongaa.*

John—   Is it an approved one?
क्या यह मान्य है?
Kyaa yaha maanaya hai?

Taxi Driver—   Yes sir, it is approved by Delhi Govt.
हाँ साहब, इसे दिल्ली सरकार ने लागू किया है।
Haan saahab, ise Delhi sarkaar ne
laagoo kiyaa hai.

John—   O.K., let us go.
ठीक है, तो फिर चलो।
Theek hai to phir chalo.

At a Hotel / होटल में

Receptionist—   Good evening sir, what can I do for you?
नमस्कार सर! मैं आपके लिए क्या कर सकती हूँ?
Namaskaar sir! main aapakee liye
kyaa kar saktee hoon?

John—   I would like to stay here for a few days.
मुझे यहाँ कुछ दिनों के लिए ठहरना है।
Mujhe yahaan kuchha dinon ke
liye theharanaa hai.

Receptionist—   Where have you come from?
आप कहाँ से आये हैं?
Aap Kahaan se aaye hain?

John—   I am from Australia.
मैं आस्ट्रेलिया से आया हूँ।
Main Australia se aayaa hoon.

Receptionist— What kind of accomodation do you need?
आपको किस तरह का कमरा चाहिये।
Aapako kis tarah ka kamara chaahiye.

John— Any comfortable room with attached bath room.
कोई भी आरामदायक कमरा जिसके साथ बाथरूम हो।
Koee bhee aarramdaayak kamaraa jiske saath bathroom ho.

Receptionist— O.K. sir, we will provide you the best room, would you like to give any special instructions.
ठीक है सर, हम आपको सबसे बढ़िया कमरा देंगे, क्या आप और कोई निर्देश देना चाहेंगे?
Theek hai sir, ham aapako sabse badhiya kamara denge. Kyaa aap aur koee nirdesh denaa chaahenge.

John— No thanks. Please send coffee to my room.
नहीं धन्यवाद! कृपया मेरे कमरे में कॉफी भेज दें।
Naheen dhanyavaad! Kripayaa mere kamare mein coffee bhej dein.

Receptionist— O.K. just sending, anything else in?
ठीक है, अभी भेजती हूँ, और कुछ चाहिए जनाब?
Theek hai, abhee bhejatee hoon, aur kuchha chaahiye janaab?

John— Thank you madam.
धन्यवाद महोदया (मैडम)।
Dhanyavaad mahodaya (madam).

Receptionist— We hope that your stay will be very comfortable here.

हम आशा करते हैं कि आप यहाँ ठहरकर बहुत खुश होंगे ।

Ham aashaa karte hain ki aap yahaan thahar kar bahut khush honge.

❑❑❑

Chapter 17

Idioms and Phrases

Common Idioms & Phrases / आम मुहावरे एवं कहावतें

1. Practice makes a man perfect
   अभ्यास से निपुणता आती है
   Abhyaas se nipuntaa aatee hai.

2. The shouts rent the sky
   आसमान नारों से गूंज उठा
   Aasmaan naaron se goonj uthaa.

3. Now a days your bread is buttered
   आजकल तुम्हारी पाँचों उंगलियाँ घी में हैं
   Aajkal tumhaaree paanchon ungleeyaan ghee mein hai1

4. We are poles apart
   हममें आकाश-पाताल का अन्तर है
   Hammein aakaash-paataal kaa antar hai.

5. He pocketed the insult
   वह आँसू पीकर रह गया
   Wah aansoo peekar raha gayaa.

6. I praised him to the skies
   मैंने उसकी तारीफ के पुल बाँध दिये
   Maine uskee taareef ke pul baandh diye.

7. The innocent are punished alongwith the guilty
गेहूं के साथ घुन भी पिसता है
Gehoon ke saath ghun bhi pistaa hai.

8. As you sow, so shall you reap
जैसी करनी, वैसी भरनी
Jaisee karnee, vaisee bharnee.

9. An empty vessel makes much noise
थोथा चना बाजे घना
Thothaa chanaa baaje ghanaa.

10. Health is wealth
सेहत हज़ार नियामत है
Sehat hazaar niyaamat hai.

11. No pain no gain
सेवा बिना मेवा नहीं
Sewaa binaa mewaa nahin.

12. Time once lost cannot be regained
गया वक्त फिर नहीं आता
Gayaa waqt phir nahin aataa.

13. Union is strength
एकता में बल है
Ektaa mein bal hai.

14. Fools praise fools
गधे को गधा खुजलाता है
Ghade ko gadhaa khujlaataa hai.

15. Barking dogs seldom bite
जो गरजते हैं वो बरसते नहीं
Jo garajte hain vo baraste nahin.

16. Where there is a will, there is a way
जहाँ चाह, वहाँ राह
Jahaan chaah, wahaan raah.

17. A bad carpenter quarrels with his tools
नाच ना जाने आंगन टेढ़ा
Naach na jaane aangan tedhaa.

18. Truth prevails
सांच को आंच नहीं
Saanch ko aanch nahin.

19. A dog is a lion in his lane
अपनी गली में कुत्ता भी शेर होता है
Apnee galee mein kuttaa bhee sher hotaa hai.

20. All's well that end's well
अन्त भले का भला
Ant bhale kaa bhalaa.

21. A friend in need is a friend indeed
मित्र वही जो मुसीबत में काम आये।
Mitra wahee jo museebat mein kaam aaye.

22. Greed is a curse
लालच बुरी बला है
Laalach buree balaa hai.

23. Tit for tat
जैसे को तैसा
Jaise ko taisaa

24. Do good find good
कर भला सो हो भला
Kar bhalaa so ho bhalaa.

25. All that glitters is not gold
हर चमकती चीज़ सोना नहीं होती
Har chamaktee cheez sonaa nahin hotee.

26. Might is right
जिसकी लाठी उसकी भैंस
Jiskee lathee uskee bhens.

27. Honesty is the best policy
ईमानदारी सबसे अच्छी नीति है
Imaandaaree sabse achchhee neeti hai.

28. Every cloud has a silver lining
वहां निराशा वहां आशा
Jahaan niraashaa wahaan aashaa.

29. To kill two birds with one stone
एक पंथ दो काज/एक तीर से दो शिकार करना
Ek panth do kaaj/Ek teer se do shikaar karnaa.

30. Great boast, little roast
नाम बड़े, दर्शन छोटे
Naam bade, darshan chhote.

31. It takes two to make quarrel
ताली एक हाथ से नहीं बजती
Taalee ek haath se nahin bajtee.

32. Slow and steady wins the race
सहज पके सो मीठा होय
Sahaj pake so meethaa hoye.

33. Do good and forget
नेकी कर दरिया में डाल
Nekee kar dariyaa mein daal.

34. Cut your coat according to your cloth
जितनी चादर देखो उतने पैर पसारो
Jitanee chaadar dekho utne pair pasaaro.

35. Truth is always bitter
सच सदा कड़वा होता है
Sach sadaa kadwaa hotaa hai.

36. Time is the greatest healer
समय सबसे बड़ा मरहम है
Samay sabse badaa marham hai.

37. Even walls have ears
दीवारों के भी कान होते हैं
Deewaaron ke bhee kaan hote hain.

38. A diamond cuts a diamond
लोहे को लोहा काटता है
Lohe ko loha kaatataa hai.

39. There are men and men, but every stone is not a gem
पाँचों अंगुलियाँ बराबर नहीं होतीं
Paanchon ongoliyaan baraabar naheen hoteen.

40. Knowledge is power
विद्या बड़ा धन है
Vidyaa badaa dhan hai.

41. There is something wrong at the bottom
दाल में कुछ काला है
Daal mein kuchha kaalaa hai.

42. God helps those who help themselves
ईश्वर उनकी सहायता करता है जो अपनी सहायता आप करते हैं
Ishwar unkee sahaaytaa kartaa hai jo apanee sahayataa aap karte hain.

43. Put cart before the horse
    उल्टा काम करना
    Ultaa kaam karnaa.

44. Where there is a rose, there is a thorn
    जहाँ फूल, वहां कांटा
    Jahaan phool, wahaan kaantaa.

45. Take the bull by the horns
    संकट का डटकर मुकाबला करना
    Sankat kaa datkar muqaabalaa karnaa.

46. Have too many irons in the fire
    एक साथ कई कामों की कोशिश करना
    Ek saath kai kaamon kee koshish karanaa.

47. Hide one's light under a bushel
    अपने गुण छिपाकर रखना
    Apne guna chhipaakar rakhanaa.

❑❑❑

Chapter 18

Adjectives / Verbs in daily use / Genders

Some Adjectives (कुछ विशेषण)

	English	हिंदी	Pronunciation
1.	Annual	वार्षिक/सालाना	*Vaarshik/ Saalaanaa*
2.	Big	बड़ा	*Badaa*
3.	Bold	निडर/साहसी	*Nidar/Saahasee*
4.	Bad	बुरा	*Buraa*
5.	Beautiful	सुन्दर	*Sundar*
6.	Brave	बहादुर	*Bahaadur*
7.	Cold	ठण्डा	*Thandaa*
8.	Coward	कायर	*Kaayar*
9.	Cruel	क्रूर/निर्दयी	*Croor/Nirdayee*
10.	Calm	शान्त	*Shaant*
11.	Clear	साफ	*Saaf*
12.	Cheap	सस्ता	*Sastaa*
13.	Deep	गहरा	*Geharaa*
14.	Dear	प्यारा/प्रिय	*Pyaaraa/Priya*
15.	Daily	रोजाना/दैनिक	*Rozaana/Dainik*
16.	Domestic	देशी	*Deshee*
17.	Dirty	गंदा	*Gandaa*
18.	Easy	आसान	*Aasaan*
19.	Fat	मोटा	*Motaa*

20.	Fast	तेज़	*Tez*
21.	False	झूठ	*Jhootha*
22.	Fresh	ताज़ा	*Taazaa*
23.	Faithful	वफ़ादार	*Vafaadaar*
24.	Golden	सुनहरा	*Suneharaa*
25.	Good	अच्छा	*Achchhaa*
26.	Greedy	लालची	*Laalachee*
27.	Heavy	भारी	*Bhaaree*
28.	Homely	घरेलू	*Ghareloo*
29.	Hard	सख़्त/कठोर/कड़ा	*Sakht/Kathor/Kadaa*
30.	Hot	गर्म	*Garam*
31.	Kind	दयालु	*Dayaalu*
32.	Long	लम्बा	*Lambaa*
33.	Large	बड़ा	*Badaa*
34.	Moody	मूडी	*Moody*
35.	Mad	पागल	*Paagal*
36.	National	राष्ट्रीय	*Raashtriya*
37.	Natural	प्राकृतिक	*Praakritik*
38.	New	नया	*Nayaa*
39.	Old	बूढ़ा	*Boodhaa*
40.	Poor	गरीब	*Gareeb*
41.	Popular	प्रसिद्ध/मशहूर	*Prasiddha/Mashahoor*
42.	Pure	शुद्ध/खरा	*Shuddha/Kharaa*
43.	Precious	कीमती/मूल्यवान	*Keematee/Moolyavaan*
44.	Rich	अमीर	*Ameer*
45.	Rural	ग्रामीण	*Graameen*
46.	Small	छोटा	*Chhotaa*
47.	Strong	मज़बूत	*Mazaboot*
48.	Short	छोटा	*Chhotaa*

	English	हिंदी	Pronunciation
49.	Sharp	पैना/नुकीला	*Painaa/Nukeelaa*
50.	Social	सामाजिक	*Saamaajik*
51.	Simple	सादा/साधारण	*Saadaa/ Saadhaaran*
52.	Thin	पतला	*Patalaa*
53.	Tall	लम्बा	*Lambaa*
54.	Tribal	जातीय	*Jaateeya*
55.	Talkative	बातूनी	*Baatoonee*
56.	Thirsty	प्यासा	*Pyaasaa*
57.	Wollen	ऊनी	*Oonee*
58.	Warm	गरम	*Garam*
59.	Weak	कमज़ोर	*Kamzor*
60.	Wise	बुद्धिमान	*Buddhimaan*
61.	Young	जवान	*Jawaan*

Verbs in Daily use / (दैनिक उपयोग की क्रियाएं)

	English	*हिंदी*	*Pronunciation*
1.	Ask	पूछना	*Poochhanaa*
2.	Boil	उबालना	*Ubaalanaa*
3.	Buy	खरीदना	*Khareedanaa*
4.	Beat	मारना/पीटना	*Maaranaa/ Peetanaa*
5.	Climb	चढ़ना	*Chadhanaa*
6.	Choose	चुनना	*Chunanaa*
7.	Call	बुलाना	*Bulaanaa*
8.	Cry	चिल्लाना	*Chillaanaa*
9.	Cut	काटना	*Kaatanaa*
10.	Catch	पकड़ना	*Pakadanaa*
11.	Carry	ले जाना/उठाना	*Le jaanaa/ Uthaanaa*

12.	Come	आना	*Aaanaa*
13.	Cook	पकाना	*Pakaanaa*
14.	Close	बंद करना	*Band karanaa*
15.	Cross	पार करना	*Paar karanaa*
16.	Dig	खोदना	*Khodanaa*
17.	Die	मर जाना	*Mara jaanaa*
18.	Drink	पीना	*Peenaa*
19.	Draw	खींचना	*Kheenchanaa*
20.	Eat	खाना	*Khaanaa*
21.	Earn	कमाना	*Kamaanaa*
22.	Finish	पूरा करना	*Pooraa karanaa*
23.	Find	मिलना/पाना	*Milanaa/Paanaa*
24.	Feel	महसूस करना	*Mehsoos karanaa*
25.	Fight	लड़ना	*Ladanaa*
26.	Fear	डरना	*Daranaa*
27.	Fall	गिरना	*Giranaa*
28.	Give	देना	*Denaa*
29.	Go	जाना	*Jaanaa*
30.	Get	पाना	*Paanaa*
31.	Invite	बुलाना	*Bulaanaa*
32.	Jump	कूदना	*Koodanaa*
33.	Kick	ठोकर मारना	*Thokar maranaa*
34.	Keep	रखना	*Rakhanaa*
35.	Know	जानना	*Jaananaa*
36.	Kill	मारना	*Maaranaa*
37.	Knock	खटखटाना	*Khatakhataanaa*
38.	Learn	सीखना	*Seekhanaa*
39.	Live	जीना	*Jeenaa*
40.	Look	देखना	*Dekhanaa*
41.	Learn	सीखना	*Seekhanaa*
42.	Laugh	हँसना	*Hansanaa*
43.	Make	बनाना	*Banaanaa*

44.	Move	हिलाना	*Hilaanaa*
45.	Marry	शादी करना	*Shaadee karanaa*
46.	Open	खोलना	*Kholanaa*
47.	Pray	प्रार्थना करना	*Prarthanaa karanaa*
48.	Play	खेलना	*Khelanaa*
49.	Push	धक्का देना	*Dhakkaa denaa*
50.	Prey	शिकार करना	*Shikaar karanaa*
51.	Plough	हल चलाना	*Hala chalanaa*
52.	Quarrel	झगड़ना	*Jhagadanaa*
53.	Run	भागना	*Bhaganaa*
54.	rise	उठना	*Uthanaa*
55.	Ride	सवारी करना	*Savaree karanaa*
56.	Receive	पाना	*Paanaa*
57.	Pick	उठाना	*Uthaanaa*
58.	Reach	पहुँचना	*Panhuchanaa*
59.	Read	पढ़ना	*Padhanaa*
60.	Sell	बेचना	*Bechanaa*
61.	Sleep	सोना	*Sonaa*
62.	Spend	खर्च करना	*Kharcha karanaa*
63.	Say	कहना	*Kehanaa*
64.	See	देखना	*Dekhanaa*
65.	Speak	कहना	*Kehanaa*
66.	Sing	गाना	*Gaanaa*
67.	Swim	तैरना	*Tairnaa*
68.	Start	शुरू करना	*Shuru karanaa*
69.	Stand	खड़ा होना	*Khadaa honaa*
70.	Sit	बैठना	*Baithanaa*
71.	Send	भेजना	*Bhejanaa*
72.	Shake	हिलाना	*Hilaanaa*
73.	Steal	चोरी करना	*Choree karanaa*
74.	Teach	पढ़ाना	*Padhaanaa*

75.	Think	सोचना	*Sochanaa*
76.	Talk	बात करना	*Baat karanaa*
77.	Take	लेना	*Lenaa*
78.	Throw	फेंकना	*Phenkanaa*
79.	Wait	इंतज़ार करना	*Intazaar karanaa*
80.	Work	काम करना	*Kaam karanaa*
81.	Weep	रोना	*Ronaa*
82.	Wear	पहनना	*Pehananaa*
83.	Wash	धोना	*Dhonaa*
84.	Wring	निचोड़ना	*Nichodanaa*
85.	Write	लिखना	*Likhanaa*

Genders / लिंग

	Masculine	*पुल्लिंग*	*Pronunciation*
1.	Actor	अभिनेता	*Abhinetaa*
2.	Author	लेखक	*Lekhaka*
3.	Boy	लड़का	*Ladakaa*
4.	Brother	भाई	*Bhaayee*
5.	Bull	बैल/सांड	*Bail/Saand*
6.	Cock	मुर्गा	*Murgaa*
7.	Dog	कुत्ता	*Kuttaa*
8.	Father	पिता	*Pitaa*
9.	Father in low	ससुर	*Sasur*
10.	Grandmather	दादा/बाबा	*Daada/Baaba*
11.	Horse	घोड़ा	*Ghoraa*
12.	Husband	पति	*Pati*
13.	Hero	वीर/नायक	*Veera/naayak*
14.	Host	मेज़बान	*Mezbaan*

15.	King	राजा	Raajaa
16.	Lion	शेर	Sher
17.	Man	आदमी	Aadmee
18.	Master	मालिक	Maalik
19.	Male	नर	Nara
20.	Nephew	भतीजा	Bhateejaa
21.	Poet	कवि	Kavi
22.	Prince	राजकुमार	Raajkumaar
23.	Son	बेटा	Betaa
24.	Uncle	चाचा/मामा	Chaachaa/ maamaa

Genders / लिंग

	Femininse	स्त्रीलिंग	Pronunciation
1.	Actress	अभिनेत्री	Abhinetree
2.	Aunt	चाची/मामी	Chaachee/Maamee
3.	Authoress	लेखिका	Lekhikaa
4.	Bitch	कुतिया	Kutiyaa
5.	Cow	गाय	Gaaya
6.	Daughter	बेटी	Betee
7.	Female	मादा	Maadaa
8.	Girl	लड़की	Ladakee
9.	Grand Mother	दादी	Daadee
10.	Heroine	वीरांगना/नायिका	Veeraanganaa/ Naayikaa
11.	Hostess	मेज़बानिन	Mezbanin
12.	Hen	मुरगी/मुर्गी	Murgee
13.	Lioness	शेरनी	Sheranee

14.	Mother	माता	*Maataa*
15.	Mistress	मालकिन	*Maalkin*
16.	Mother in law	सास	*Saas*
17.	Mare	घोड़ी	*Ghoree*
18.	Niece	भतीजी	*Bhateejee*
19.	Poetess	कवयित्री	*Kavayitree*
20.	Princess	राजकुमारी	*Raajkumaaree*
21.	Queen	रानी	*Raanee*
22.	Sister	बहन	*Bahan*
23.	Wife	पत्नी	*Patnee*
24.	Woman	औरत	*Aurat*

❏❏❏

Chapter 19

Similar Words having different meanings

Similar Words having different meanings / एकसमान किंतु अलग अर्थ देने वाले शब्द

English	हिंदी	Pronunciation
1. Accept	स्वीकार करना	*Sweekaar karnaa*
Except	अतिरिक्त/अलावा	*Atirikt/Alawaa*
Expect	आशा करना	*Aashaa karnaa*
2. Access	पहुँच	*Pahunch*
Excess	बहुत ज्यादा	*Bahut Zyaadaa*
3. Advice	सलाह	*Salaaha*
Advise	सलाह देना	*Salaaha denaa*
4. Affect	असर/प्रभाव	*Asara/Prabhaava*
Effect	नतीज़ा/परिणाम	*Nateezaa/Parinaam*
5. Alter	बदलना	*Badalnaa*
Altar	पूजा की जगह	*Pooja kee jagaha*
6. Ascent	चढ़ना	*Chadhanaa*
Assent	सहमति	*Sahamati*

7.	Adapt	अनुकूल बनाना	*Anukool banaanaa*
	Adopt	अपनाना⁄गोद लेना	*Apanaanaa/Goda*
8.	Addition	जोड़ना⁄बढ़ाना	*Jodanaa/Badhaanaa*
	Edition	संस्करण (पुस्तक	*Sansakaran (Pustak*
	(of book)	का)	*kaa)*
9.	Amend	संशोधन	*Sanshodhan*
	Emend	सुधारना	*Sudhaaranaa*
10.	Adverse	प्रतिकूल⁄विरुद्ध	*Pratikool/Viruddha*
	Averse	अनिच्छुक	*Anichchhuk*
11.	Bail	जमानत	*Jamaanat*
	Bale	गठरी	*Gatharee*
12.	Bear	भालू	*Bhaaloo*
	Bear	सहन करना	*Sahan karnaa*
	Bare	खाली⁄नंगा	*Khaalee/Nangaa*
13.	Birth	जन्म	*Janma*
	Berth	सोने की सीट	*Sone kee seat*
	(in train)	(गाड़ी में)	*(gaadee main)*
14.	Bridal	वैवाहिक	*Vaivaahik*
	Bridle	लगाम	*Lagaam*
15.	Bazaar	बाज़ार⁄मार्किट	*Baazaar/Market*
	Bizarre	अनोखा⁄बेतुका	*Anokhaa/Betukaa*

	English	Hindi	Transliteration
16.	Born	पैदा/उत्पन्न होना	*Paidaa/Utpanna honaa*
	Borne	उठाना	*Uthaanaa*
17.	Breath	साँस	*Saansa*
	Breathe	साँस लेना	*Saansa lenaa*
	Breadth	चौड़ाई	*Chaudaaee*
18.	Beside	समीप/पास	*Sameep/paas*
	Besides	के अतिरिक्त/अलावा	*Ke atirikt/Alaawaa*
19.	Cannon	बंदूक/तोप	*Bandook/Topa*
	Canon	नियम/कानून	*Niyam/Kanoon*
20.	Cast	फेंकना	*Phenkanaa*
	Caste	जाति	*Jaati*
21.	Cession	प्रदान	*Pradaan*
	Session	बैठक	*Baithaka*
22.	Cattle	मवेशी	*Maveshee*
	Kettle	केतली	*Ketalee*
23.	Check	जाँचना/रोकना	*Janchanaa/Rokanaa*
	Cheque	बैंक का चैक	*Bank kaa cheque*
24.	Cite	उल्लेख करना	*Ullekha karanaa*
	Site	स्थान	*Sthaan*
	Sight	दृष्टि/दृश्य	*Drishti/Drishya*
25.	Colonel	सेना में ऑफिसर	*Senaa main officer*
	Kernel	गिरी/दाना	*Giree/Daanaa*

26.	Coarse	खुरदरा	*Khurdaraa*
	Course	पाठ्यक्रम/प्रक्रिया	*Pathyakram/ Prakriyaa*
27.	Council	परिषद/समिति	*Parishad/Samiti*
	Counsel	परामर्श	*Paraamarsh*
28.	Complement	पूरक	*Poorak*
	Compliment	प्रशंसा	*Prashansaa*
29.	Cease	बंद करना	*Banda karanaa*
	Seize	पकड़ना	*Pakadanaa*
30.	Cent	सिक्का (सेंट)	*Sikkaa (cent)*
	Scent	इत्र	*Itra*
31.	Childish	बचकाना	*Bachakaanaa*
	Childlike	भोलाभाला	*Bholaabhaalaa*
32.	Decease	मृत्यु/मौत	*Mrityu/Maut*
	Disease	बीमारी	*Beemaaree*
33.	Dissent	असहमति	*Asahamatee*
	Descent	नीचे आना	*Neeche Aanaa*
34.	Defer	स्थगित करना	*Sthagit karnaa*
	Differ	अन्तर होना	*Antar honaa*
35.	Desert	रेगिस्तान	*Registaan*
	Dessert	मीठा (भोजन के बाद)	*Meethaa (Bhojan ke baad)*

36.	Dew	ओस	*Osa*
	Due	देय	*Deya*
37.	Die	मरना	*Maranaa*
	Dye	रंगाना	*Rangaanaa*
38.	Draft	खाका/रूपरेखा	*Khaakaa/Rooparekhaa*
	Draught	खुराक	*Khuraaq*
	Drought	सूखा	*Sookhaa*
39.	Diary	डायरी	*Diary*
	Dairy	दुग्धशाला/डेरी	*Dugdhashaalaa/Dairy*
40.	Deference	सम्मान	*Sammaan*
	Difference	अन्तर	*Antar*
41.	Dual	दुगुना	*Dugunaa*
	Duel	दोनों	*Donon*
42.	Dose	दवाई	*Dawaaee*
	Doze	ऊँघना	*Oonghanaa*
43.	Expand	फैलना	*Failanaa*
	Expend	खर्च करना	*Kharcha karanaa*
44.	Eligible	योग्य/पात्र	*Yogya/Paatra*
	Illigible	अस्पष्ट/अपाठ्य	*Aspashata/Apaathaya*
45.	Eminent	श्रेष्ठ/ऊँचा	*Shreshtha/Oonchaa*
	Imminent	सन्निकट	*Sannikat*

46.	Fair	साफ़/सुन्दर/मेला	*Saaf/Sunder/Melaa*
	Fare	किराया	*Kiraayaa*
47.	Feet	नापने का पैमाना (फुटा)	*Naapane kaa paimaanaa (Futaa)*
	Feet	पैर	*Pair*
	Feat	असाधारण कार्य	*Asaadhaarana kaarya*
48.	Floor	फ़र्श	*Farsh*
	Flour	आटा	*Aataa*
	Flower	फूल	*Phool*
49.	Facility	सुविधा	*Suvidhaa*
	Felicity	खुशी	*Khushee*
50.	Forth	आगे	*Aage*
	Fourth	चौथा	*Chauthaa*
51.	Farther	दूर	*Door*
	Further	आगामी	*Aagaamee*
52.	Gait	चाल	*Chaala*
	Gate	दरवाज़ा	*Darwazaa*
53.	Hale	स्वस्थ	*Swastha*
	Hail	ओले/स्वागत	*Ole/Swaagat*
54.	Heel	एड़ी	*Aidee*
	Heal	ठीक होना	*Theek honaa*

55.	Hoard	जमा करना/संचय	*Jamaa karanaa/* *Sanchaya*
	Horde	झुंड/गिरोह	*Jhunda/Giroha*
56.	Human	मनुष्य/मानव	*Manushaya/Maanav*
	Humane	दयालु	*Dayaaloo*
57.	Honorany	अवैतनिक	*Avaitanik*
	Honourable	आदर योग्य	*Aadar Yogya*
58.	Holy	पवित्र	*Pavitra*
	Wholly	सम्पूर्ण रूप से	*Sampoorna roop se*
59.	Idle	बेकार	*Bekaar*
	Idol	मूर्ति	*Moorti*
	Ideal	आदर्श	*Aadarsha*
60.	Lessen	कम करना	*Kama karanaa*
	Lesson	पाठ	*Paatha*
61.	Lightening	रोशनी करना	*Roshanee karanaa*
	Lightning	बिजली चमकना	*Bijalee chamkanaa*
62.	Lose	खोना	*Khonaa*
	Loose	ढीला	*Dheelaa*
63.	Last	अन्तिम	*Antim*
	Latest	नवीनतम	*Naveentam*
64.	Mail	डाक	*Daak*
	Male	नर/पुरुष/आदमी	*Nar/Purush/Aadamee*

65.	Merry	खुशी/प्रसन्नता	*Khushee/Prasanataa*
	Marry	शादी करना	*Shaadee karanaa*
66.	Minor	नाबालिग/अव्यस्क	*Naabaalig/Avayaska*
	Miner	खनिक	*Khanik*
67.	Metal	धातु	*Dhaatu*
	Mettle	उत्साह/साहस	*Utsaah/Saahas*
68.	Medal	मैडल/पदक	*Medal/Padak*
	Middle	बीच में	*Beech mein*
69.	Moral	नैतिक शिक्षा	*Naitik shikshaa*
	Morale	मनोदशा/हौसला	*Manodashaa/Hausalaa lenaa*
70.	Naughty	शरारती	*Sharaaratee*
	Knotty	मुश्किल	*Mushakil*
71.	Ordinance	अध्यादेश	*Addhayaadesha*
	Ordnance	तोपखाना	*Topakhaanaa*
72.	Pail	बाल्टी	*Baaltee*
	Pale	पीला	*Peelaa*
73.	Plain	सादा	*Saadaa*
	Plane	समतल/वायुयान	*Samatala/Vaayuyaan*
74.	Personal	व्यक्तिगत	*Vyaktigat*
	Personnel	कर्मचारी (स्टाफ)	*Karmacharee (staff)*

75. Principal   मुख्य/प्रधान   *Mukhaya/Pradhaan*
    Principle   नियम/सिद्धांत   *Niyam/Siddhaant*

76. Quite   बिल्कुल   *Bilkul*
    Quiet   चुपचाप   *Chupachaapa*

77. Root   जड़   *Jada*
    Rout   हार/दंगा   *Haar/Dangaa*
    Route   रास्ता   *Raastaa*

78. Rain   वर्षा/बरसात   *Varashaa/Barasaat*
    Reign   शासन करना   *Shaasan karanaa*
    Rein   बागडोर   *Baagador*

79. Sealing   मुहरबंदी   *Muharbandee*
    Ceiling   भीतरी छत   *Bheetaree chhata*

80. Story   कहानी   *Kahaanee*
    Storey   मंज़िल   *Manzil*

81. Sure   निश्चित   *Nishichit*
    Sour   खट्टा/कटु   *Khattaa/Katu*
    Sore   दुखना   *Dukhanaa*
    Soar   उड़ना   *Udanaa*
    Shore   किनारा   *Kinaaraa*

82. Straight   सीधा   *Seedhaa*
    Strait   तंग/कठिन   *Tung/Kathin*

83. Stationery   लेखन-सामग्री   *Lekhan-saamagree*
    Stationary   स्थिर   *Sthir*

84.	Suit	सूट/प्रार्थना/मुकदमा	*Suit/Prarthanaa/Muquadamaa*
	Suite	कमरों का सेट	*Kamaron kaa set*
	Soot	काजल	*Kaajal*
85.	Temper	स्वभाव/क्रोध	*Swabhaava/Krodha*
	Tamper	थापी	*Thaapee*
86.	Team	दल/समूह/टोली	*Dala/Samooha/Tolee*
	Teem	भरा हुआ	*Bharaa huaa*
87.	Vale	अलविदा/घाटी	*Alavidaa/Ghaatee*
	Veil	घूंघट/पर्दा	*Ghoonghat/Pardaa*

❑❑❑

Chapter 20

Some More Expressions

Some more Expressions / कुछ और अभिव्यक्तियां

1. Apple of one's eye
   बहुत प्रिय होना
   Bahut priya honaa.

2. All of a sudden
   अचानक ही
   Achaanak hee.

3. All at once
   अचानक
   Achaanak.

4. Absent minded person
   लापरवाह व्यक्ति
   Laaparwaah vyakti.

5. At random
   अन्धाधुन्ध
   Andhaadhundh.

6. A red letter day
   खास दिन
   Khaas din.

7. A white elephant
दिखावे की चीज़
Dikhaave kee cheez.

8. At the eleventh hour
अन्तिम क्षण में
Antim kshana mein.

9. Birds of a feather
एक ही स्वभाव के लोग
Ek hee swabhaav ke log.

10. Black sheep
बदनाम आदमी/कुलकलंक
Badnaam aadmee/kulkalank.

11. Bad blood
दुश्मनी
Dushmanee.

12. Bad of roses
सुख की स्थिति
Sukh kee stithee.

13. Blue stocking
विदुषी स्त्री
Vidushee stiree.

14. Bosom friend
जिगरी दोस्त
Jigaree dost.

15. By heart
अच्छी तरह याद करना
Achchhee taraha yaad karnaa.

16. Build casttes in the air
ख्याली पुलाव पकाना / हवाई किले बनाना
Khyaalee pulav pakaanaa/Hawaaee kile banaanaa.

17. By leaps and bounds
दिन दूनी रात चौगुनी
Din doonee raat chaugunee.

18. Crocodile tears
बनावटी आँसू
Banaavati ansoo.

19. Cry over spilt milk
बेकार ही खेद करना
Bekaar hee khed karnaa.

20. Capital idea
बेमिसाल विचार
Bemisaal vichaar.

21. Cock and bull story
बनावटी कहानी
Banaavatee kahaanee.

22. Crux of a problem
समस्या की जड़
Samasyaa kee jad.

23. Dead of night
आधी रात को
Aadhee raat ko.

24. Draw the line
सीमा तय करना
Seemaa taya karnaa.

25. Dead tired
बहुत थका होना
Bahut thakaa honaa.

26. Eat one's word
बात से पीछे हटना
Baat se peechhe hatanaa.

27. Fellow feeling
भाईचारा/अपनापन
Bhaaeechaaraa/Apnaapan.

28. Fan the flames
आग में घी डालना
Aag mein ghee daalnaa.

29. Get rid of
छुटकारा पाना
Chhutkaaraa paanaa.

30. Get by heart
जबानी याद करना
Zabaanee yaad karnaa.

31. Get into hot water
मुश्किल में पड़ना
Mushkil mein padanaa.

32. Go through fire and water
कोई भी खतरा मोल लेना
Koi bhee khatraa mol lenaa.

33. Golden opportunity
सुनहरा मौका/बहुत अनुकूल अवसर
Suneharaa maukaa/Bahut anookool avsar.

34. Good deal
अच्छा सौदा
Achchhaa saudaa.

35. Grow grey
एक ही काम में जीवन बिताना
Ek hee kaam mein jeewan bitaanaa.

36. Good humour
खुशमिजाज़
Khushmijaaz.

37. Hall mark
श्रेष्ठ होना
Kshreshtha honaa.

38. Hush money
रिश्वत
Rishwat.

39. Hard of hearing
कम सुनना
Kama sunnaa.

40. Herculean task
बहुत कठिन कार्य
Bahut kathin kaarya.

41. Hand to mouth
मुश्किल से गुजारा
Mushkil se gujaaraa.

42. In vain
बेकार में
Bekaar mein.

43. In full swing
बहुत जोरों से
Bahut joron se.

44. Idle compliment
झूठी तारीफ
Jhothee taareef.

45. In the same boat
एक जैसी परिस्थिति में होना
Ek jaisee paristithi mein honaa.

46. In time
समय पर
Samaya par.

47. Iron will
पक्का इरादा
Pakkaa iraadaa.

48. Jack of all trades
सब काम कर सकने वाला
Sab kaam kar sakne waalaa.

49. Keep an eye on
निगरानी रखना
Nigraanee rakhnaa.

50. Keep in the dark
जानकारी ना देना
Jaankaaree naa denaa.

51. Kick a habit
आदत छोड़ देना
Aadat chhod denaa.

52. Leave in the lurch
मुश्किल में साथ छोड़ देना
Mushkil mein saath chhod denaa.

53. Let the cat out of the bag
भेद खोलना
Bhed kholnaa.

54. Lion's share
बहुत बड़ा हिस्सा होना
Bahut badaa hissaa honaa.

55. Make a hash
गड़बड़ घोटाला करना
Gadbad ghotaalaa karanaa.

56. Make fun of
किसी का मजाक उड़ाना
Kisee kaa mazaak udaanaa.

57. Make both ends meet
आय में मुश्किल से गुज़ारा कर पाना
Aaya mein mushkil se guzaaraa kar paanaa.

58. Make neither head nor tail
कुछ भी समझ न आना
Kuchchha bhee samajh na aanaa.

59. Man in thousand
बहुत अच्छा आदमी
Bahut achchhaa aadamee.

60. Man in the street
आम आदमी
Aam aadmee.

61. Middle age (between 40 to 60)
बीच की आयु (चालीस से साठ तक)
Beecha kee aayu (between 40 to 60 years).

62. Miss the boat
अवसर खोना
Avasar khonaa.

63. Mind one's own business
अपना काम करना
Apnaa kaam karnaa.

64. Move heaven and earth
बहुत अधिक कोशिश करना
Bahut adhik koshish karnaa.

65. Naked eye
नंगी आँख से
Nangee aankh se.

66. Narrow escape
बाल-बाल बचना
Baal baal bachnaa.

67. Never mind
कोई बात नहीं
Koee baat nahin.

68. Nip in the bud
शुरू में ही खत्म कर देना
Shuroo mein hee khatam kar denaa.

69. Nine day's wonder
थोड़े दिनों का आकर्षण
Thode dinon kaa aakarshan.

70. Not fit to hold a candle
निचले दर्ज़े का होना
Nichale darze kaa honaa.

71. Not worth his salt
नालायक व्यक्ति
Naalaayak vyakati.

72. Oily tongue
खुशामद की भाषा
Khushaamad kee bhaashaa.

73. Open hearted man
खुले दिल का आदमी
Khule dil kaa aadmee.

74. Open handed man
खुला खर्च करने वाला आदमी
Khulaa kharch karne waalaa aadmee.

75. Out of order (instrument/machine)
खराब (यंत्र/मशीन)
Kharaab (yantra/machine).

76. Out of date
पुराना
Puraanaa.

77. Out of pocket
जेब से ज्यादा
Jeb se jyaadaa.

78. Pick holes
गलतियाँ निकालना
Galtiyaan nikaalnaa.

79. Pink of condition
    उत्तम स्वास्थ्य होना
    Uttam swasthya honaa.

80. Queer fish
    अस्थिर व्यक्ति
    Asthir vyakti.

81. Red handed
    रंगे हाथ
    Range haath.

82. Short cut
    नज़दीक का रास्ता
    Nazdeek kaa raastaa.

83. Sink or swim
    करो या मरो
    Karo yaa maro.

84. Snake in the grass
    आस्तीन का साँप
    Aasteen kaa saanp.

85. Split hairs
    बारीक फर्क निकालना
    Baareeq fark nikaalnaa.

86. Time hangs heavy
    मुश्किल में समय निकालना
    Mushkil mein samaya nikaalnaa.

87. Up to date
आधुनिक
Aadhunik.

88. Up and downs
उतार-चढ़ाव
Uttaar chadhaav.

89. Wolf in sheep's clothing
धोखेबाज़ मित्र
Dhokhebaaz mitra.

❑❑❑

Chapter 21

Indian States and Capitals / Union Territories / Statewise Official Languages / 50 Big Cities of India

India is a federal union of 28 states and 7 union territories grouped into 5 major regions: North, Mid India, South, East and NorthEast. India is always a centre of attraction for tourists. From the high ranges of Himalayas to the great blue Indian ocean, it is full of natural beauty, colourful culture and variety of people. It has different languages, a large number of big cities with popular tourists spots.

Moreover, every state has a large selection of famous traditional dishes also. Being a country of scenic beauty and majestic cultural diversity as well as its ancient royal heritage, these all makes India a very attractive destination for worldwide tourism. In this chapter, some common key information words for touriests are given, which are divided under the suitable headings.

Indian States and Capitals / भारतीय राज्य और राजधानियाँ

	State	राज्य	Capital	राजधानी
1.	Andhra Pradesh	आंध्र प्रदेश	Hyderabad	हैदराबाद
2.	Arunachal Pradesh	अरुणाचल प्रदेश	Itanagar	ईटानगर
3.	Assam	असम	Dispur	दिसपुर
4.	Bihar	बिहार	Patna	पटना
5.	Chhattisgarh	छत्तीसगढ़	Raipur	रायपुर
6.	Goa	गोवा	Panaji	पणजी
7.	Gujarat	गुजरात	Gandhinagar	गांधीनगर
8.	Haryana	हरियाणा	Chandigarh	चंडीगढ़
9.	Himachal Pradesh	हिमाचल प्रदेश	Shimla	शिमला
10.	Jammu & Kashmir	जम्मू व कश्मीर	Srinagar	श्रीनगर
11.	Jharkhand	झारखंड	Ranchi	रांची
12.	Karnataka	कर्नाटक	Bengaluru	बेंगलुरु
13.	Kerela	केरल	Thiruvananthapuram	तिरुअनंतपुरम

14.	Madhya Pradesh	मध्य प्रदेश	Bhopal	भोपाल
15.	Maharashtra	महाराष्ट्र	Mumbai	मुंबई
16.	Manipur	मणिपुर	Imphal	इंफाल
17.	Meghalaya	मेघालय	Shilong	शिलांग
18.	Mizoram	मिजोरम	Aijawl	आइज़ोल
19.	Nagaland	नागालैंड	Kohima	कोहिमा
20.	Orissa	उड़ीसा	Bhubaneswar	भुवनेश्वर
21.	Punjab	पंजाब	Chandigarh	चंडीगढ़
22.	Rajasthan	राजस्थान	Jaipur	जयपुर
23.	Sikkim	सिक्किम	Gangtok	गंगटोक
24.	Tamil Nadu	तमिलनाडु	Chennai	चेन्नई
25.	Tripura	त्रिपुरा	Agartala	अगरतला
26.	Uttar Pradesh	उत्तर प्रदेश	Lucknow	लखनऊ
27.	Uttarakhand	उत्तराखंड	Dehradun	देहरादून
28.	West Bengal	पश्चिम बंगाल	Kolkata	कोलकाता

Union Territories (संघशासित प्रदेश)

	Union Territories	संघशासित प्रदेश	Capital	राजधानी
1.	Andaman & Nicobar Islands	अंडमान और निकोबार द्वीपसमूह	Port Blair	पोर्ट ब्लेयर
2.	Chandigarh	चंडीगढ़	Chandigarh	चंडीगढ़
3.	Dadra and Nagar Haveli	दादरा और नगर हवेली	Silvassa	सिलवासा
4.	Daman and Div	दमन और दीव	Daman	दमन
5.	Lakshadweep	लक्षद्वीप	Kavaratti	कावारत्ती
6.	National Capital Territory of Delhi	राष्ट्रीय राजधानी क्षेत्र दिल्ली	Delhi	दिल्ली
7.	Puducherry	पुडुच्चेरी	Puducherry	पुडुच्चेरी

Statewise Official Languages (राज्यवार राजभाषाएं)

	State	Official langauages	राजभाषाएं
1.	Andhra Pradesh	Telgu/Urdu	तेलुगु/उर्दू
2.	Arunachal Pradesh	Assamese/English	असमिया/अंग्रेजी
3.	Assam	Assamese/Bodo	असमिया/बोडो
4.	Bihar	Hindi/Maithili/Urdu	हिंदी/मैथिली/उर्दू
5.	Chhattisgarh	Hindi/Chhattisgarhi	हिंदी/छत्तीसगढ़ी
6.	Goa	Konkani	कोंकणी
7.	Gujarat	Gujarati/Hindi	गुजराती/हिंदी
8.	Haryana	Hindi	हिंदी
9.	Himachal Pradesh	Hindi/Pahari	हिंदी/पहाड़ी
10.	Jammu & Kashmir	Urdu	उर्दू
11.	Jharkhand	Hindi/Santali	हिंदी/संथाली
12.	Karnataka	Kannada	कन्नड़
13.	Kerela	Malayalam/English	मलयालम/अंग्रेजी

14.	Madhya Pradesh	Hindi	हिंदी
15.	Maharashtra	Marathi	मराठी
16.	Manipur	Manipuri	मणिपुरी
17.	Meghalaya	Khasi/Garo/English	खासी/गारो/अंग्रेजी
18.	Mijoram	Mizo	मिज़ो
19.	Nagaland	English	अंग्रेजी
20.	Orissa	Odia	ओड़िया
21.	Punjab	Punjabi	पंजाबी
22.	Rajasthan	Hindi/Rajasthani	हिंदी/राजस्थानी
23.	Sikkim	Nepali	नेपाली
24.	Tamil Nadu	Tamil	तमिल
25.	Tripura	Bengali/Kokborok/English	बंगाली/काकबोरोक/अंग्रेजी
26.	Uttar Pradesh	Hindi/Sanskrit/Urdu	हिंदी/संस्कृत/उर्दू
27.	Uttarakhand	Hindi/Urdu	हिंदी/उर्दू
28.	West-Bengal	Bengali/Nepali	बंगाली/नेपाली

Official Languages of Union Territories
(संघशासित प्रदेशों की राजभाषाएं)

	Union Territories	Office Languages	राजभाषाएं
1.	Andaman & Nicobar Islands	Hindi/Tamil/Telugu/ Bengali/English	हिंदी/तमिल/तेलुगु/ बंगाली/अंग्रेजी
2.	Chandigarh	Punjabi/Hindi/English	पंजाबी/हिंदी/अंग्रेजी
3.	Dadra and Nagar Haveli	Marathi/Gujarati	मराठी/गुजराती
4.	Daman and Diu	Gujarati/Marathi/English	गुजराती/मराठी/अंग्रेजी
5.	Delhi	Hindi/Urdu/Punjabi/English	हिंदी/उर्दू/पंजाबी/अंग्रेजी
6.	Lakshadweep	Malayalam	मलयालम
7.	Puducherry	Tamil/English/French/ Malayalam/Telugu	तमिल/अंग्रेजी/फ्रेंच मलयालम/तेलुगु

50 Big Cities of India (भारत के 50 बड़े शहर)

	Name of City	शहर का नाम	State
1.	Agra	आगरा	Uttar Pradesh
2.	Ahemadabad	अहमदाबाद	Gujarat
3.	Allahabad	इलाहाबाद	Uttar Pradesh
4.	Amritsar	अमृतसर	Punjab
5.	Asansol	आसनसोल	West Bengal
6.	Aurangabad	औरंगाबाद	Maharashtra
7.	Bangaluru	बेंगलुरू	Karnataka
8.	Bhopal	भोपाल	Madhya Pradesh
9.	Bhubaneswar	भुवनेश्वर	Orissa
10.	Chandigarh	चंडीगढ़	UT Chandigarh
11.	Chennai	चेन्नई	Tamil Nadu
12.	Coimbatore	कोयंबटूर	Tamil Nadu
13.	Delhi	दिल्ली	UT Delhi
14.	Dhanbad	धनवाद	Jharkhand
15.	Guwahati	गुवाहाटी	Assam
16.	Gwaliar	ग्वालियर	Madhya Pradesh
17.	Hyderabad	हैदराबाद	Andhra Pradesh
18.	Indore	इंदौर	Madhya Pradesh
19.	Jabalpur	जबलपुर	Madhya Pradesh
20.	Jaipur	जयपुर	Rajasthan
21.	Jamshedpur	जमशेदपुर	Jharkhand
22.	Jodhpur	जोधपुर	Rajasthan
23.	Kanpur	कानपुर	Uttar Pradesh
24.	Kochi	कोच्ची	Kerela

25.	Kolhapur	कोल्हापुर	*Maharashtra*
26.	Kolkata	कोलकाता	*West-Bengal*
27.	Kozhikode	कोषीकोड	*Kerela*
28.	Lucknow	लखनऊ	*Uttar Pradesh*
29.	Ludhiana	लुधियाना	*Punjab*
30.	Madurai	मदुरै	*TamilNadu*
31.	Meerut	मेरठ	*Uttar Pradesh*
32.	Mumbai	मुंबई	*Maharashtra*
33.	Nagpur	नागपुर	*Maharashtra*
34.	Nashik	नाशिक	*Maharashtra*
35.	Patna	पटना	*Bihar*
36.	Pune	पुणे	*Maharashtra*
37.	Raipur	रायपुर	*Chhattisgarh*
38.	Rajkot	राजकोट	*Gujarat*
39.	Ranchi	रांची	*Jharkhand*
40.	Sagar	सागर	*Madhya Pradesh*
41.	Solapur	सोलापूर	*Maharashtra*
42.	Srinagar	श्रीनगर	*Jammu & Kashmir*
43.	Surat	सूरत	*Gujarat*
44.	Thiruvananthapuram	तिरूअनंतपुरम	*Kerela*
45.	Tiruchirappalli	तिरूचिरापल्ली	*Tamil Nadu*
46.	Ujjain	उज्जैन	*Madhya Pradesh*
47.	Vijayvada	विजयवाड़ा	*Andhra Pradesh*
48.	Varanasi	वाराणसी	*Uttar Pradesh*
49.	Vadodara	वडोदरा	*Gujarat*
50.	Visakhapatnam	विशाखापटनम	*Andhra Pradesh*

❑❑❑

Chapter 22

Famous IndianTourist Spots: Places/Attractions/Monuments/Hill Stations/Beaches/Religious Sites

Place / स्थान

Top 10 Places	10 प्रमुख स्थान	State
1. Agra	आगरा	Uttar Pradesh
2. Panjim	पणजी	Goa
3. Jaipur	जयपुर	Rajasthan
4. Srinagar	श्रीनगर	Jammu & Kashmir
5. Mussorie	मसूरी	Uttrakhand
6. Udaipur	उदयपुर	Rajasthan
7. Darjeeling	दार्जीलिंग	West Bengal
8. Shatiniketan	शांतिनिकेतन	West Bengal
9. Allahabad	इलाहाबाद	Uttar Pradesh
10 Khajuraho	खजुराहो	Madhya Pradesh

Attractions / आकर्षण

Top 10 Attractions	10 प्रमुख आकर्षण	State
1. Tajmahal	ताजमहल	Agra
2. Goa	गोवा	Panjim
3. Kerela & Backwaters	केरल	Kerela

4.	Beaches	सागर तट	*Goa & Kerala*
5.	Himalayas	हिमालय	*North India*
6.	Khajuraho Temples	खजुराहो के मंदिर	*Madhya Pradesh*
7.	Varanasi Ghats	वाराणसी के घाट	*Uttar Pradesh*
8.	Ajanta or Allora Caves	अजंता व एलोरा की गुफाएं	*Maharashtra*
9.	Ganges River	गंगा नदी	*Uttrakhand*
10	Corbett National Park	कार्बेट नेशनल पार्क	*Uttrakhand*

❑❑❑

Monuments of India (भारत के स्मारक)

Name of Monument	स्मारक का नाम	City/State
1. Agra Fort	आगरा का किला	Agra/Uttar Pradesh
2. Ajanta & Allora Caves	अजंता व एलोरा की गुफाएं	Aurangabad/Maharashtra
3. Amer Fort	आमेर का किला	Jaipur/Rajasthan
4. Amravati Stupa	अमरावती का स्तूप	Amaravati/Maharashtra
5. Charminar	चारमीनार	Hyaderabad/Andhra Pradesh
6. Chattisgarh Fort	चित्तौड़ का किला	Chittorgarh/Rajasthan
7. CST-Mumbai	सीएसटी-मुंबई	Mumbai/Maharashtra
8. Dilwara Temples	दिलवाड़ा के मंदिर	Mount Abu/Rajasthan
9. Elephanta Caves	एलीफेंटा की गुफाएं	Mumbai/Maharashtra
10 Fatehpur Sikri	फतहपुर सीकरी	Fatahpur/Uttar Pradesh
11. Gateway of India	गेटवे ऑफ इंडिया	Mumbai/Maharashtra
12. Gwalior Fort	ग्वालियर का किला	Gwaliar/Madhya Pradesh

13.	Gol Gumbad	गोल गुंबद	*Bijapur /Karnataka*
14.	Golconda Ford	गोलकोंडा का किला	*Hyderabad/Andhra Pradesh*
15.	Golden Temple	स्वर्ण मंदिर	*Amritsar/Punjab*
16.	Hawa Mahal	हवा महल	*Jaipur/Rajasthan*
17.	India Gate	इंडिया गेट	*Delhi/UT Delhi*
18.	Jama Masjit	जामा मस्जिद	*Delhi/UT Delhi*
19.	Jantar Mantar	जंतर-मंतर	*Delhi/UT Delhi*
20	Khajuraho Temples	खजुराहो के मंदिर	*Khajuraho/Madhya Pradesh*
21.	Lake Palace	लेक पैलेस	*Udaipur/Rajasthan*
22.	Lotus Temple	लोटस टेंपल	*Delhi/UT Delhi*
23.	Mahabodhi Temple	महाबोधि मंदिर	*Gaya/Bihar*
24.	Qutub Minar	कुतुब मीनार	*Delhi/UT Delhi*
25.	Red Fort	लाल किला	*Delhi/UT Delhi*
26.	Sanchi Stupa	सांची के स्तूप	*Sanchi/Bihar*
27.	Shri Meenakshi Temple	श्री मीनाक्षी मंदिर	*Madurai/Tamil Nadu*

28.	Somnath Mandir	सोमनाथ मंदिर	*Somnath/Gujarat*
29.	Sun Temple	सूर्य मंदिर	*Kanark/Orissa*
30.	Taj Mahal	ताजमहल	*Agra/Uttar Pradesh*
31.	Tirupathi Temple	तिरुपति मंदिर	*Tirupati/Andhra Pradesh*
32.	Ummaid Bhawan Palace	उम्मेद भवन पैलेस	*Jodhpur/Rajasthan*
33.	Victoria Memorial	विक्टोरिया मेमोरियल	*Kolkata/West Bengal*
34.	Vidhan Saudha	विधान सौध	*Bangalura/Karanataka*
35.	Warangal Fort	वारंगल का किला	*Warrangal/Andhra Pradesh*

Indian Hill Stations (भारत के पहाड़ी स्थान)

Station	स्थान	City/State
1. Almora	अल्मोड़ा	*Uttar Pradesh*
2. Badrinath	बद्रिनाथ	*Uttar Pradesh*
3. Bhimtal	भीमताल	*Uttarakhand*
4. Chail	चैल	*Himachal Pradesh*

5.	Chamba	चम्बा	*Himachal Pradesh*
6.	Coonoor	कोन्नूर	*Kerela*
7.	Dalhausie	डलहौजी	*Himachal Pradesh*
8.	Darjeeling	दार्जिलिंग	*West Bengal*
9.	Dharamshala	धर्मशाला	*Himachal Pradesh*
10.	Gangotri	गंगोत्री	*Uttar Pradesh*
11.	Gulmurg	गुलमर्ग	*Jammu & Kashmir*
12.	Kalimpong	कालिम्पोंग	*Sikkim*
13.	Kangra	कांगड़ा	*Himachal Pradesh*
14.	Kasauli	कसौली	*Himachal Pradesh*
15.	Khandala	खंडाला	*Maharashtra*
16.	Kodaikanal	कोडइकनाल	*Tamil Nadu*
17.	Kufri	कुफरी	*Himachal Pradesh*
18.	Kullu	कुल्लू	*Himachal Pradesh*
19.	Ladakh	लद्दाख	*Jammu & Kashmir*
20.	Lonavala	लोणावला	*Maharashtra*

21.	Mahabaleshwar	महाबलेश्वर	*Maharashtra*
22.	Manali	मनाली	*Himachal Pradesh*
23.	Matheran	माथेरान	*Maharashtra*
24.	Mirik	मिरिक	*West Bengal*
25.	Mount Abu	माउंट आबू	*Rajasthan*
26.	Mussoorie	मसूरी	*Uttar Pradesh*
27.	Nainital	नैनिताल	*Uttarakhand*
28.	Ooty	ऊटी	*Karanataka*
29.	Pachmarhi	पचमढ़ी	*Madhya Pradesh*
30.	Pahalgam	पहलगाम	*Jammu & Kashmir*
31.	Panchgani	पंचगनी	*Maharashtra*
32.	Ranikhet	रानीखेत	*Uttrakhand*
33.	Shillong	शिलांग	*Assam*
34.	Shimla	शिमला	*Himachal Pradesh*
35.	Srinagar	श्रीनगर	*Jammu & Kashmir*

Beaches of India (भारत के सागर तट)

	Name of Beach	तट का नाम	State
1.	Andaman Nicobar	अंडमान निकोबार	UT Andaman Nicobar
2.	Anjuna	अंजुना	Goa
3.	Baga	बागा	Goa
4.	Calangute	कालंगूट	Goa
5.	Chandipur	चांदीपुर	Orissa
6.	Chawpatti	चौपाटी	Maharashtra
7.	Colva Beach	कोलवा बीच	Goa
8.	Dona Paula	दोना पउला	Goa
9.	Ganapatipule	गणपतिपुले	Maharashtra
10.	Juhu Beach	जुहू बीच	Maharashtra
11.	Kanyakumari	कन्याकुमारी	Tamila Nadu
12.	Kavaratti	कावारात्ती	Lakshadweep
13.	Kovalam	कोवलम	Kerela
14.	Mangalore	मैंगलोर	Karnataka
15.	Marina	मरीना	Tamil Nadu
16.	Marve Manori Gorai	मार्वे मनोरी गोराई	Maharashtra
17.	Miramar	मीरामर	Goa
18.	Murud Janjira	मुरूड जंजीरा	Maharashtra
19.	Porbander	पोरबंदर	Gujarat
20	Puri Beach	पुरी तट	Orissa
21.	Rameshwaram	रामेश्वरम	Tamil Nadu
22.	Somnath	सोमनाथ	Gujarat

23.	Udupi	उडुपी	*Karnataka*
24.	Vagator	वागाटोर	*Goa*
25.	Veraval Beach	वेरावल तट	*Gujarat*

Indian Religious Sites (भारत के धार्मिक स्थल)

	Name of Site	*स्थान का नाम*	*State*
1.	Ajmer	अजमेर	*Rajasthan*
2.	Akshardham	अक्षरधाम	*Gujarat*
3.	Allahabad	इलाहाबाद	*Uttarakhand*
4.	Amarnath	अमरनाथ	*Jammu & Kashmir*
5.	Amritsar	अमृतसर	*Punjab*
6.	Badrinath	बद्रीनाथ	*Uttar Pradesh*
7.	Bhubaneswar	भुवनेश्वर	*Orrisa*
8.	Bodhgaya	बोधगया	*Bihar*
9.	Chitrakoot	चित्रकूट	*Uttar Pradesh*
10.	Dwarka	द्वारका	*Gujarat*
11.	Gangotri & Yamnotri	गंगोत्री व यमनोत्री	*Uttar Pradesh*
12.	Goa	गोवा	*Goa*
13.	Haridwar	हरिद्वार	*Uttrakhand*
14.	Hemkunt Sahib	हेमकुंड साहिब	*Uttrakhand*
15.	Kanyakumari	कन्याकुमारी	*Tamil Nadu*
16.	Kapilvastu	कपिलवस्तु	*Bihar*
17.	Kedarnath	केदारनाथ	*Uttar Pradesh*
18.	Konark	कोणार्क	*Orissa*
19.	Lumbini	लुम्बिनी	*Bihar*

20	Madurai	मदुरै	*Tamil Nadu*
21.	Mathura	मथुरा	*Uttar Pradesh*
22.	Nalanda	नालंदा	*Bihar*
23.	Patna Sahib	पटना साहिब	*Bihar*
24.	Puri	पुरी	*Orrissa*
25.	Puttaparthi	पुट्टापर्थी	*Andhra Pradesh*
26.	Rameshwaram	रामेश्वरम	*Tamil Nadu*
27.	Rishikesh	ॠषिकेष	*Uttar Pradesh*
28.	Sarnath	सारनाथ	*Bihar*
29.	Shirdi	शिरडी	*Maharashtra*
30.	Sravanbelagola	श्रावणबेलगोला	*karnataka*
31.	Thanjavur	तंजावुर	*Kerela*
32.	Tirupati	तिरूपति	*Andhra Pradesh*
33.	Vaishno Devi	वैष्णो देवी	*Jammu & Kashmir*
34.	Varanasi	वाराणसी	*Uttar Pradesh*
35.	Vrindavan	वृंदावन	*Uttar Pradesh*

❑❑❑

Chapter 23

State and Regionwise Popular Foods, Dishes and Some Famous Indian Sweets

Name of Food/ Dish	भोजन/पकवान का नाम	State
Northern Region		
1. Rogan Josh	रोगन जोश	*Jammu & Kasmir*
2. Dum Aloo	दम आलू	*Jammu & Kasmir*
3. Kahava (Green Tea)	कहवा (हरी चाय)	*Jammu & Kasmir*
4. Makki Roti & Sarson ka Saag	मक्की रोटी व सरसों का साग	*Punjab*
5. Rajma Chawal	राजमा चावल	*Punjab*
6. Chholey & Bhature	छोले व भटूरे	*Punjab*
7. Dal Makkhani	दाल मक्खनी	*Punjab*
8. Kulche & Chholey	कुलचे व छोले	*Punjab*
9. Sooji Halwa (Parsad)	सूजी हलवा (प्रसाद)	*Punjab*
10 Lassi (Whipped Yogurt)	लस्सी (बिलोया दही)	*Punjab*
11. Kachri Subji	कचरी की सब्जी	*Haryana*
12. Cholia	छोलिया	*Haryana*
13. Chhachh (buttermilk)	छाछ (मट्ठा)	*Haryana*

14.	Bajra Khichri	बाजरे की खिचड़ी	*Haryana*
15.	Dal-Bati-Choorma	दाल-बाटी-चूरमा	*Rajasthan*
16.	Lal Maas	लाल मांस	*Rajasthan*
17.	Besan Gatta	बेसन गट्टा	*Rajasthan*
18.	Piyaj Kachori	प्याज की कचौरी	*Rajasthan*
19.	Aloo Gutke	आलू गुटके	*Uttarakhand*
20	Jhangora Kheer	झंगोरा खीर	*Uttarakhand*
21.	Shami Kabab	शामी कबाब	*Uttar Pradesh*
22.	Awadh Biryani	अवध बिरयानी	*Uttar Pradesh*
23.	Aloo Kachori	आलू कचौरी	*Uttar Pradesh*
24.	Moong Dal Halwa	मूंग दाल हलवा	*Uttar Pradesh*
25.	Benaras Chaat	बनारस की चाट	*Uttar Pradesh*

Mid India

1.	Lapsi	लापसी	*Madhya Pradesh*
2.	Bhutte Kheer	भुट्टे की खीर	*Madhya Pradesh*
3.	Bhopali Kabab	भोपाली कबाब	*Madhya Pradesh*
4.	Thepla	थेपला	*Gujarat*
5.	Dhokla	ढोकला	*Gujarat*
6.	Khandvi	खांडवी	*Gujarat*
7.	Nankhatai	नानखताई	*Gujarat*
8.	Thali	थाली	*Maharashtra*
9.	Vada Pao	वड़ा पाव	*Maharashtra*
10	Modak	मोदक	*Maharashtra*
11.	Upma	उपमा	*Maharashtra*
12.	Missal	मिसल	*Maharashtra*

13. Ussal	ऊसल	*Maharashtra*
14. Vindaloo	विन्दालू	*Goa*
15. Xacuti	ज़कुटी	*Goa*
16. Bibinca	बिबिन्का	*Goa*
17. Praun Balchao	प्राउन बालचाओ	*Goa*

South India

1. Bisi Bele Bhaat	बिसी बेल भात	*Karnataka*
2. Kesari Bath	केसरी बथ	*Karnataka*
3. Mysore Pak	मैसूर पाक	*Karnataka*
4. Sadya Meal	सद्य मील	*Kerela*
5. Avial	एवॉयल	*Kerela*
6. Malabar Parotha	मालाबार परोठा	*Kerela*
7. Hyderabadi Biryani	हैदराबादी बिरयानी	*Andhra Pradesh*
8. Mirchi Salan	मिर्ची सालन	*Andhra Pradesh*
9. Ghongura Pickle	घोंगुरा आचार	*Andhra Pradesh*
10 Uttapam	उत्तपम	*Tamil Nadu*
11. Masala Dosa	मसाला दोसा	*Tamil Nadu*
12. Idli-Sambhar	इडली-सांभर	*Tamil Nadu*
13. Rasam	रसम	*Tamil Nadu*
14. Pongal	पोंगल	*Tamil Nadu*
15. Vada-Sambhar	वड़ा-सांभर	*Tamil Nadu*
16. Dal Vada	दाल वड़ा	*Tamil Nadu*
17. Kadugu Yerra	कडुगु येरा	*Puducherry*

North East Region

1.	Litti	लिट्टी	*Bihar*
2.	Sattu	सत्तू	*Bihar*
3.	Khaja	खाजा	*Bihar*
4.	Tilkut	तिलकुट	*Bihar*
5.	Thekua	थेकुआ	*Jharkhand*
6.	Pua	पुआ	*Jharkhand*
7.	Marua Roti	मरूआ रोटी	*Jharkhand*
8.	Momos	मोमो	*Sikkim*
9.	Thukpa	थुकपा	*Sikkim*
10	Sael Roti	सइल रोटी	*Sikkim*
11.	Apong (Beer)	अपोंग (बीयर)	*Arunachal*
12.	Maasor Tenga	मासौर टेंगा	*Assam*
13.	Pitha	पिठा	*Assam*
14.	Momos	मोमोज़	*Nagaland*
15.	Rice Beer	चावल बीयर	*Nagaland*
16.	Cherry Wine	चैरी वाइन	*Nagaland*
17.	Iromba	इरोम्बा	*Manipur*
18.	Kabok	काबोक	*Manipur*
19.	Chakkauba	चकाऊबा	*Manipur*
20	Jadoh	जाडो	*Meghalaya*
21.	Kyat (Beer)	कयात (बीयर)	*Meghalaya*
22.	Chakhwi	चखबी	*Tripura*
23.	Makhavi	मखबी	*Tripura*
24.	Muitru	मुइत्रू	*Tripura*
25.	Zu (Tea)	जू	*Mizoram*

East India

1.	Bhapa Lish	भापा लिश	*West Bengal*
2.	Mishti Doi (Sweet Yogurt)	मिष्टी दोई (मीठा दही)	*West Bengal*
3.	Machhli Jhoal	मछली झोल	*West Bengal*
4.	Fish Orly	मछली ओरली	*Orissa*
5.	Khirmohan	खीरमोहन	*Orissa*

Delhi Special

1.	Papdi Chaat	पापड़ी चाट
2.	Paratha	परांठा
3.	Choley & Bhature	छोले व भटूरे
4.	Seenkh Kabab	सींख कबाब
5.	Haleem	हलीम
6.	Korma Tikka	कोरमा टिक्का
7.	Muttun Masala	मटन मसाला
8.	Chicken Tandoori	चिकन तंदूरी
9	Golgappe	गोलगप्पे
10.	Aaloo Chaat	आलू चाट
11.	Falooda-Rabri	फलूदा-रबड़ी
12.	Stuffed Nan	भरवां नान
13.	Kulche-Chholey	कुलचे-छोले
14.	Bedmi Puri	बेड़मी पूरी

Famous Indian Sweets (भारत की मशहूर मिठाइयां)

Name of Sweet	मिठाई का नाम	Name of Sweet	मिठाई का नाम
Angoori Petha	अंगूरी पेठा	Kamarcut	कमरकट
Bal Mithai	बाल मिठाई	Karadantu	करादांतु
Balushahi	बालूशाही	Khaja	खाजा
Barfi	बरफी	Kheer	खीर
Basundi	बासुंदी	Kheer Kadam	खीर कदम
Besan Burfi	बेसन बरफी	Kheersagar	खीरसागर
Boorelu	बूरेलु	Khurma	खुरमा
Chamcham	चमचम	Kobbari Lavaju	कोबारी लवाजू
Chhena Geja	छेना गाजा	Kulfi	कुल्फी
Chhena Kheeri	छेना खीरी	Laddu	लड्डू
Chena Jalebi	छेना जलेबी	Langcha	लांगचा
Chkki	चिक्की	Malai Laddu	मलाई लड्डू
Coconut Burfi	नारियल बरफी	Milk Cake	मिल्क केक

Dharwad Pedha	धारवाड. पेड़ा	Neyyappam	नेयाप्पम
Doda	डोडा	Pantua	पंटुआ
Double ka Meetha	डबल का मीठा	Peda	पेड़ा
Ghevar	घेवर	Petha	पेठा
Gulab Jamun	गुलाब जामुन	Pauan Poli	पूरन पोली
Halwa	हलवा	Qubani ka Meetha	खुबानी का मीठा
Imartee	इमरती	Ras Malai	रस मलाई
Jaangiri	जांगीरी	Rasgulla	रसगुल्ला
Jalebi	जलेबी	Sandesh	संदेश
Jhajariya	झाजरिया	Sheer Korma	शीर कोरमा
Kaju Katli	काजू कतली	Shirini	शिरिनी
Kaju Burfi	काजू बरफी	Shrikhand	श्रीखंड
Kalakand	कलाकंद	Tilgul	तिलगुल
Kaala Jam	काला जाम	Tilkut	तिलकूट
Singori	सिंगोरी	Unniappam	उन्नीअप्पम
Sohan Halwa	सोहन हलवा		
Sohan Papdi	सोहन पापड़ी		

Other Books on
LANGUAGE BOOKS

1. Learn to Speak and Write Arabic

2. Teach Yourself Spanish

3. Learn to Speak and Write Russian

4. Learn to Speak and Write Korean

5. French Made Easy

6. Learn to Speak and Write Hindi

7. Learn to Speak and Write Italian

8. Conversational Chinese

9. Learn to Speak and Write French

10. Learn to Speak and Write German

11. Learn to Speak and Write Spanish

12. Learn to Speak and Write Japanese

Lotus PRESS

Unit No. 220, 2nd Floor, 4735/22, Prakash Deep Building,
Ansari Road, Darya Ganj, New Delhi- 110002
Ph. : 41325510, 9811838000
E-mail : lotuspress1984@gmail.com, www.lotuspress.co.in